Effective
FORTRAN 77

Effective
FORTRAN 77

Michael Metcalf
CERN, Geneva, Switzerland

CLARENDON PRESS · OXFORD

Oxford University Press, Walton Street, Oxford OX2 6DP

Oxford New York Toronto
Delhi Bombay Calcutta Madras Karachi
Petaling Jaya Singapore Hong Kong Tokyo
Nairobi Dar es Salaam Cape Town
Melbourne Auckland

and associated companies in
Berlin Ibadan

Oxford is a trade mark of Oxford University Press

Published in the United States
by Oxford University Press, New York

First published 1985
Reprinted (with corrections) 1986, 1987, 1989

British Library Cataloguing in Publication Data
Metcalf, Michael
Effective FORTRAN 77.
1. FORTRAN (Computer program language)
2. Microcomputer—Programming
I. Title
001.64'24 QA76.73.F25
ISBN 0–19–853709–3

Library of Congress Cataloging in Publication Data
Metcalf, Michael.
Effective FORTRAN 77.
Bibliography: p.
Includes index.
1. FORTRAN (Computer program language)   I. Title
QA76.73.F25M478   1985   001.64'24   84–28522
ISBN 0–19–853709–3

Printed in Great Britain by
St. Edmundsbury Press Ltd.
Bury St Edmunds, Suffolk

PREFACE

FORTRAN 77 is now established as the dominant version of this programming language, relegating FORTRAN 66 to the position of a computing relic. The introduction of the new standard in the late 1970s led to the publication of a spate of excellent text books, but these are usually intended for beginners — those who have no experience, either in FORTRAN or in programming as such. This means that more experienced FORTRAN programmers are often left to their own devices, as there are very few texts which enable them to revise and develop their skills. At the same time, there are very many programmers who begin their training in BASIC or in a teaching language such as PASCAL, and are confronted with FORTRAN only later when they embark on their careers in research or industry.

The purpose of this book is to provide a complete but concise review of the FORTRAN 77 programming language, to serve both as a reference for the intermediate or advanced programmer, and as a means whereby programmers in other languages can rapidly acquire a knowledge of FORTRAN 77, without becoming bogged down in expanses of explanatory text more suitable for absolute beginners. The book should similarly be useful to FORTRAN 66 programmers wishing to convert to the new standard, and to those beginners who may prefer a faster approach to the topic. However, the book goes beyond a bare exposition of the language, presenting other material which helps in an understanding of its history and development, as well as giving detailed advice on how FORTRAN should be used wisely within the boundaries of its inherent limitations. Since FORTRAN, the first high-level programming language, is a far from perfect tool, it is even more important that it be used carefully, lacking as it does much of the built-in protection contained in more recent languages.

Chapter 1 gives a brief introduction to computers and a short review of FORTRAN's relatively long and successful history, as well as indicating likely developments in the future. The following six chapters are devoted to a complete description of the language. They present the version defined by the 1978 ANSI standard, the reader being taken step-by-step through each of its features, which are explained in sufficient but not excessive detail.

At a time when the interchange of software is becoming ever more important and computer systems ever more varied, it is essential to ensure that programs written and tested on one system will run with little or no change on another. Chapter 8 provides a list of recommendations which should help in the production of portable code. Writing portable code from the outset can often save costly re-programming at a later stage, and is a technique which needs to be absorbed when learning the language itself.

The topics of style and good programming practice are further developed in Chapter 9, and the question of program design is tackled in Chapter 10, which shows how the principles of good program design can be applied in the context of FORTRAN programming.

One of FORTRAN's prime advantages has always been its emphasis on efficient object program execution, and some advice on how this might be achieved is given in Chapter 11. As modern computers become more powerful, the problems they help to solve become more complex, and it remains vital to ensure that programs remain efficient, even though computer hardware is ever cheaper.

The final chapter, 12, deals briefly with the topics of program testing and documentation, two areas neglected in many texts, but ones which are important in program development and maintenance.

FORTRAN has had a long and successful history and, in spite of the development of new languages, it still remains the most widely used in large-scale scientific computation. This book does not set out to demonstrate that it is a perfect tool for that purpose, but rather tries to ensure that it is used to the best possible effect in those areas in which it still has no obvious contender.

ACKNOWLEDGEMENTS

A book such as this contains a great deal of detailed information which requires extensive and careful checking. I have been greatly helped in this task by several friends and colleagues, and I am particularly grateful to J. M. Gerard and R. Matthews of CERN and to J. D. Wilson of Leicester University for their critical comments on drafts of the text. The responsibility for any remaining errors or omissions is entirely my own.

Much of the advice in the latter half of the book has been collected from diverse sources, and I acknowledge particularly the work of Mme. F. Vapne of the Electricite de France, which provided the basis of Chapters 8 and 9. I thank also the University of Leicester for permission to reproduce Appendix B.

It is a pleasure to thank the CERN management, and especially P. Zanella, for encouraging me to undertake this work, and for providing the necessary resources for its realisation.

My final thanks go to A. Berglund and D. Stungo for their helpful cooperation in the preparation of the final camera-ready copy.

CONTENTS

1 INTRODUCING FORTRAN

This book is concerned with the FORTRAN programming language. It sets out not only to offer a complete and relatively concise description of the whole language, but seeks also to emphasise those language features which are considered to be consistent with good programming practice. Features which are less desirable are given less prominence. The language description occupies Chapters 2 to 7, which are written in such a way that simple programs can already be coded after the first three of these chapters have been read. Successively more complex programs can be written as the information in each subsequent chapter is absorbed. Chapter 7 covers the whole of the input/output features in a manner which confines the more advanced features to its end, so that the reader can approach this more difficult area feature by feature, but always with a useful subset behind him.

The remainder of the book is concerned with the effective use of the language. It sets out to provide guidance which goes beyond the coding of syntactically correct programs, describing how programs can also be made portable, neat, efficient, well documented and tested. Although these chapters may often read as long lists of do's and don'ts, they provide the material necessary to progress from a mere formal command of the language to the ability to wield it as a well mastered tool.

This present chapter has the task of setting the scene for those which follow. For those who are unfamiliar with any notions of computers or computing, it contains a very brief and highly simplified description of the basic hardware elements out of which computers are constructed, and goes on to present some basic concepts of computer programs and programming. Since this book is aimed at readers who typically already have some familiarity with programming, these two sections may be skipped by such people without loss.

The remaining three sections of this introductory chapter present the FORTRAN language as such. FORTRAN has evolved considerably since it was first introduced about thirty years ago, and these sections describe its history, current status and likely future, this last section being inevitably somewhat speculative.

1. Computer Hardware

A large computer is one of the most complex and ingenious pieces of machinery ever devised by man. Fortunately, the typical programmer has to understand rather little about its inner workings, and can often write small-scale programs without great concern for what goes on behind the scenes, although most large-scale applications require more detailed knowledge of the capabilities and limitations of the hardware.

1.1 Storage

Computing is concerned with the manipulation or processing of *data*. These data may be lists of numbers, school records, company accounts, airline schedules, or any other kind of information suitable for automatic processing. In order to have the data available in a form in which it may be readily accessed, every computer has a *main memory* or *store*. A store is normally divided into *words,* each word containing one item of information, as shown in Fig. 1. The number of words in a store varies from several thousand on very small microprocessors, to several hundred million on large super-computers.

Each word in the store is composed of more elementary units known as *bits*. A bit can have only one of two values, 0 or 1, often represented physically by the on or off state of a minute electronic switch. If a word contains m bits, then the word itself can be in any of 2^m different states. The actual meaning assigned to a particular pattern of 0's and 1's in a word depends on the individual computer model, but almost all computers store the positive integers, 0, 1, 2, 3 *etc.* in a way whereby each bit which is set to 1 in the word represents a value which is $2^{(n-1)}$, where n is the position of the bit within the word counting from the right. The number 14 can thus be represented by the bit string 1110, *i.e.* the sum of $2^{(2-1)}$, $2^{(3-1)}$ and $2^{(4-1)}$, or pictorially:

$$\boxed{0}\boxed{0}\boxed{0}\boxed{0}\boxed{0}\boxed{0}\boxed{0}\boxed{0}\boxed{0}\boxed{0}\boxed{0}\boxed{0}\boxed{1}\boxed{1}\boxed{1}\boxed{0}$$

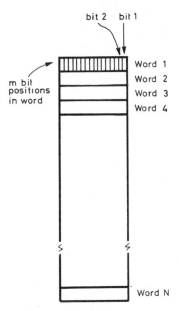

Fig. 1 A computer store

Many present day computers have stores with 32 bits to a word, with an intermediate division of the word into four groups of eight contiguous bits. Such a group of eight bits is known as a *byte*. A byte has 2^8 or 256 different states, and may be used to store, for instance, the different representations of the characters in a character set of upper and lower case letters, numbers, punctuation marks *etc*.

Access to words in main memory is fast, but the memory itself is expensive. Since the amount of data a computer is expected to process often far exceeds the capacity of the main memory to store it, there is usually another level of storage which has a much larger capacity, but is less expensive per unit of storage. This is known as a backing store, and on most modern computer systems consists of various types of rotating disc packs. This type of storage has the drawback that the access to the data is slower than for main memory.

A further level of storage is provided by magnetic tapes, which have to be physically mounted onto units before they can be written or read, but which are very cheap, and each can hold quantities of data exceeding thousands of millions of bits.

We thus see that there is a hierarchy of storage, from small, fast but expensive main memory, to large, slow but cheap dismountable tapes. A further level on many computers is a small, high-speed memory known as a *cache memory* which acts as a buffer between the rest of the storage system and the device which exploits it, the central processing unit.

1.2 Central processing unit

The heart of a computer is its central processing unit (CPU). This is the device which performs the actual processing of the data. For instance, it may take the contents of two specified locations in memory, add them together and return the result to a third location. To be able to perform this operation, the operands will be fetched from memory and placed in high-speed *registers* in the CPU. These are a small store of usually a few dozen words inside the CPU itself, to which access is extremely fast, allowing the CPU to operate on their contents at its full speed, without having to wait for operands to be fetched from main memory, once they have been placed in the registers.

The main part of the CPU is the arithmetic and logic unit (or units), which is a device capable of performing various *operations* on *operands* held in the registers. These operations are the familiar arithmetic operations of add, multiply, subtract and divide, as well as others which, for example, allow the bits of a word to be shifted in position to the left or right, to be complemented, masked or to be logically combined with the bits of another word. A CPU and its registers are shown diagrammatically in Fig. 2, and a fuller description of several actual models can be found in Metcalf (1982).

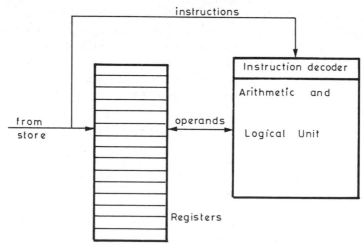

Fig. 2 A central processing unit

1.3 Instructions

A CPU has not only to be supplied with data, but also requires the necessary orders on how the data are to be manipulated. These orders are contained in *instructions* which consist of coded information about which operands are to be operated on, and by which operators. The instructions control directly the movement of data words between the main memory and the registers in the CPU.

The instructions themselves are stored just like data words in the main memory. In many computers, a special register points to the location in memory which contains the next instruction to be executed. When the current instruction has been carried out, the next instruction word is fetched from memory into a special part of the CPU, where it is first decoded, and the orders it contains then executed. This is also shown in Fig. 2. Since at the level of the storage an instruction word is treated just like a data word, it is perfectly possible for the CPU to modify instructions stored in memory.

1.4 Access to a computer

Nowadays there are two principal ways in which computers are used and accessed. In the first, the computer is relatively small, and sits on a desk top or in a corner of an office, and is operated interactively *via* a *visual display unit* or *terminal*. This consists of a keyboard which may be used to send *commands* to the computer, and a screen on which the computer displays requests for commands and the responses to those requests. The operation of the terminal may be under direct control of the CPU of the computer to which it is connected, or be controlled indirectly by other hardware.

The second method of use is once again *via* a terminal, but in this case the computer to which it is connected is located remotely, possibly in the same building but perhaps many kilometers away. Here, the computer in question will be larger, and there may be as many as several hundred people using it simultaneously. The connection between the terminals and the large computer will often be under control of smaller computers. In many cases, a number of large computers will be linked together in a *network,* or be connected *via* telephone lines, and it will be possible for a user sitting at his terminal to connect from one computer to another, and even to use a computer situated in another country or continent.

2. Computer Software

The computer hardware which has just been outlined operates under the control of sequences of instructions. These instructions are stored in memory, and fetched by the CPU for decoding and execution. A long sequence of instructions might be only partially stored in main memory, the remainder being kept in the backing store until needed. A sequence of instructions to perform a defined task is known as a *program*. A collection of programs to control the operation of the hardware of a computer and of the application programs submitted by users is known as an *operating system*.

Programs are written in a precisely defined code, or *programming language*. These exist in various forms. Those languages which require a detailed knowledge of the hardware of a specific computer are known as *low-level languages*. Others written in a more abstract way requiring little or no such knowledge are called *high-level languages*. FORTRAN is such a language. It is written in a manner akin to mathematical formulae, and is translated into the instructions required to drive the CPU by another program which is part of the operating system and known as a *compiler*. The compiler reads the FORTRAN *source code*, checks that the syntax is correct, *i.e.* that it conforms to the rules of FORTRAN grammar, and generates the instructions in the form of a so-called *object code*. In order for this code to be executed, it must first be correctly placed in the computer's memory and the execution initiated. This is the task of other programs, which are also part of the operating system and known as *loaders* and *linkage-editors*.

Programs are collectively known as computer software. A given piece of hardware − or computer − can in principle be operated and used by many different suites of software. In practice, very few different operating systems exist for a given type of computer, as it requires a large investment in manpower and hence money to write such a system. Application programs to solve a small problem, on the other hand, may often be written in an afternoon by one person, although very large application programs are also written, comparable in size and complexity to an operating system. In this book, we shall be concerned with just one language used to write application programs varying in size from a few lines to hundreds of thousands of lines.

3. How FORTRAN Began

Programming in the early days of computing was tedious in the extreme. Programmers required a detailed knowledge of the instructions, registers and other aspects of the CPU of the computer for which they were writing code. The *source code* itself was written in a mysterious shorthand in which the bits of each instruction word were grouped in threes, so called *octal code*. In the course of time mnemonic codes were introduced, a form of coding known as *machine* or *assembly code*. These codes were translated into the instruction words by programs known as *assemblers*. In the 1950's it became increasingly apparent that this form of programming was highly inconvenient, if only because of the length of time required to write and test a program, although it did enable the CPU to be used in a very efficient way.

These difficulties spurred a team led by John Backus of IBM to develop the first ever high-level language, FORTRAN (Backus, 1957). Their aim was to produce a language which would be simple to understand but almost as efficient in execution as assembly language. In this they succeeded beyond their wildest dreams. The language was indeed simple to learn, as it was possible to write mathematical formulae almost as they are usually written in mathematical texts. (In fact, the name FORTRAN is a contraction of Formula Translation). This enabled working programs to be written five times faster than before, for a loss in efficiency of only about 20 percent in execution time. This was achieved by devoting a great deal of care to the construction of the first ever compiler, a considerable achievement as new ground had to be broken at every step. We thus see that FORTRAN was an innovation, not only as the first high-level language, but also due to the fact that it gave rise to a branch of computer science, now known as the theory of compilers.

But FORTRAN was revolutionary as well as innovatory. Programmers were relieved of the tedious burden of using assembler language, and were able to concentrate more on the problem in hand. Perhaps more important, however, was the fact that computers became accessible to any scientist willing to devote a little effort to acquiring a working knowledge of FORTRAN; no longer was it necessary to be an expert on computers to be able to write application programs.

FORTRAN spread rapidly as it fulfilled a real need. By 1964 there were 43 different compilers running on 16 systems. Inevitably dialects of the language developed, which led to problems in exchanging programs between computers, and so in 1966, after four years' work, the then American Standards Association (later the American National Standards Institute, ANSI) brought out the first ever standard for a programming language, now known as FORTRAN 66, (but also sometimes as FORTRAN IV).

FORTRAN brought with it several other advances, apart from its ease of learning combined with a stress on efficient execution of code. It was, for instance, a language which remained close to, and exploited, the available hardware rather than being an abstract concept. It also brought with it, *via* the EQUIVALENCE statement (see Section 5.5), the possibility for programmers to control storage allocation in a simple way, a feature which was very necessary in those early days of small memories, even if it is frowned upon nowadays as being potentially dangerous. Lastly, the source code did not depend on any blank characters in its syntax, freeing the programmer from the duty of writing code in rigidly defined columns, and allowing him to lay out the code in almost any way he wished, within the constraints of the FORTRAN source form. As implied already, not all these advances are still regarded as desirable.

4. FORTRAN's Present Status

The proliferation of dialects mentioned in the previous section became a problem, once again, after the publication of the 1966 standard. A first difficulty was that many compilers did not even adhere to the standard. A comparison of six compilers carried out in 1970 revealed that the *only* statement implemented with neither extensions nor contradictions to the standard was the unconditional GOTO statement.

A second difficulty was the wide-spread implementation in compilers of features which were essential for large-scale programs, but which were not mentioned at all by the standard. An example of this was error handling, *i.e.* the ability of a program to recover gracefully from the various hardware faults which it might encounter such as exceeding the allowed central processor time or calculating the square-root of a negative number. Every compiler implemented such facilities in a way different from all others.

This situation, combined with the existence of some evident flaws in the language, resulted in the introduction of large numbers of so-called *pre-processors*. These are programs which are able to read in the source code of some well-defined extended dialect of FORTRAN and to generate a second text in standard FORTRAN which is then be presented to the FORTRAN compiler in the usual way. This provided a means for extending FORTRAN, yet still retaining the ability to transport the transformed source code from one computer to another. Pre-processors also represented a means whereby new language features could be tested, without having to go to the lengths necessary to incorporate them into a proper compiler. At the same time, the large number of such pre-processors meant that there was an even greater diversity of high-level dialects in use. Although programs written using a pre-processor could be exchanged at the FORTRAN source level, the automatically generated FORTRAN code was often unacceptably difficult to read.

These difficulties were partially resolved by the publication of a new standard, known as FORTRAN 77 (ANSI, 1978). Some far-sighted manufacturers, such as DEC, decided to introduce compilers conforming to the new standard as rapidly as possible. Others, notably IBM, seemed very reluctant to make the move, and brought out usable products only about five years later. This meant that the transition period between FORTRAN 66 and FORTRAN 77 was much longer than it should have been, and that the two standards have had to coexist for a considerable time, resulting evidently in a yet greater diversity of FORTRAN dialects.

By 1984, however, the changeover to FORTRAN 77 seemed to be in full swing, and FORTRAN 66 code was being phased out rapidly. Manufacturers began to stop supporting the old compilers, thus increasing the pressure to change. Whilst it was a relatively simple matter to write new code under the new standard, converting old code was easy only to the extent that the old standard had been adhered to, as there is a large measure of compatibility between the two standards. On the other hand, programs which had used many of the old extensions were often difficult to convert, as the new compilers are often stricter than the old, and do not necessarily always include the former extensions.

It is the purpose of this book to explain the FORTRAN 77 standard with no extensions whatsoever, and indeed even to indicate certain standard features as being undesirable so that a slightly smaller version of the language is recommended. In this way portable programs can be written from the outset. Chapter 8 is devoted to a summary of hints on portability, and only there are certain common extensions mentioned, in order to warn the unwary that they are not standard features.

5. The Future of FORTRAN

After thirty years' existence, FORTRAN is far from being the only programming language available on most computers. In the course of time new languages have been developed, and where they were demonstrably more suitable for a particular type of application they have been adopted in preference to FORTRAN for that purpose. FORTRAN's superiority has always been in the area of numerical, scientific, engineering and technical applications, and there is still no significant competitor in these fields. That does not mean, however, that the FORTRAN community is necessarily completely content with the language, and in order that it be brought properly up-to-date, an ANSI committee is once again preparing a new standard, presently known as FORTRAN 8x. This is fully described in Metcalf and Reid (1987).

Unlike the previous standard, which resulted from an effort to standardize *existing practices,* the new standard will be much more a *development* of the language, introducing many features which are completely new to FORTRAN, although nearly all of them are based on experience in other languages. The most significant new feature will be the ability to handle arrays of numbers using a concise but powerful notation. This will lead to a simplification in the coding of many mathematical problems, and will also make FORTRAN a more efficient language on the new generation of super-computers as these array features are well matched to their hardware. An introduction to super-computers is given in Metcalf (1982).

The new standard will incorporate so many features which are tailor-made to the needs of its users that it is difficult to imagine that FORTRAN will ever cease to be used in those application areas where it presently has such clear advantages, at least for a very long time to come.

2 LANGUAGE ELEMENTS

1. Introduction

Written prose in a natural language, such as an English text, is composed firstly of basic elements − the letters of the alphabet. These are combined into larger entities, words, which convey the basic concepts of objects, actions and qualifications. Examples are the words 'apple', 'eat' and 'red', respectively. The words of the language can be further combined into larger units, phrases and sentences, according to certain rules. One set of rules defines the grammar. This tells us whether a certain combination of words is correct in that it conforms to the *syntax* of the language, that is those acknowledged forms which are regarded as correct renderings of the meanings we wish to express. For instance, the combination *'I apple eat the red'* is just a jumble which has no meaning beyond that of correctly spelt individual words, whereas *'I eat the red apple'* expresses the operation of eating performed by a person, I, on a certain object, an apple, of a particular type, red.

Another set of rules is that of style. These rules go further than the rules of grammar, in that they assume that the grammar is correct, and provide guidance on how meaning can be conveyed in a way which is clear, precise and appropriate. Meaning should not be obscured by imprecise vocabulary, nor should understanding be hampered by clumsy grammatical constructions. Style is a function of the context. A botanist would use a more precise word for 'apple', and a poet might prefer a more evocative adjective for 'red'.

Sentences can in turn be joined together into paragraphs, which conventionally contain the composite meaning of their constituent sentences, each paragraph expressing a larger unit of information. In a novel, sequences of paragraphs become chapters and the chapters together form a book, which usually is a self-contained work, largely independent of all other books.

2. Character Set

Analogies to all these concepts are found in a programming language. In FORTRAN, the basic elements, or character set, are the 26 upper-case letters of the English alphabet, the 10 Arabic numerals, 0 to 9, and the 13 so-called special characters listed in Table 1.

Table 1

The special characters of the FORTRAN language

Character Symbol	Name
=	Equals sign
+	Plus sign
−	Minus sign
*	Asterisk
/	Slash
(	Left parenthesis
)	Right parenthesis
,	Comma
.	Decimal point
$	Currency symbol
'	Apostrophe
:	Colon
	Blank

In the course of this and the following chapters, we shall see how further analogies with natural language may be drawn. The unit of FORTRAN information is the *statement*. Statements, like sentences, may be joined to form larger units like paragraphs. In FORTRAN these are know as *blocks,* which are well-defined only in certain cases. Blocks of FORTRAN statements may be grouped into units known as *program units* (chapters in our analogy), and out of these may be built a complete *program,* which forms a complete set of instructions to a computer to carry out a pre-defined sequence of operations on specified data. The simplest program may consist of only a few statements, but programs of more than 100,000 statements are now quite common.

Such large programs, like books, are made more understandable if they are written in a style which aids rather than hinders a reader's comprehension of their meaning and purpose, and in this book stress will be laid upon style and not just upon the mere provision of explanations of the FORTRAN grammar.

Within the context of FORTRAN, the letters and numerals may be combined into certain sequences which have one or more meanings. For instance, one of the meanings of the sequence 999 may be a constant in the mathematical sense. We shall encounter other interpretations of this type of sequence later. Similarly, the sequence DATE might represent, as one possible interpretation, a variable quantity to which we assign the calendar date.

The special characters also have various meanings. We shall see how the asterisk is used to specify the operation of multiplication, as in X*Y, and has also a multitude of other interpretations.

In the FORTRAN language, the characters have a property not found in natural languages, known as a *collating sequence*. This property implies that the characters are an ordered set, so that one may ask the question whether one character occurs before or after another in the sequence. This question is posed in a natural form such as *'Is C less than M?'*, and we shall see later how this may be expressed in FORTRAN terms. FORTRAN possesses no full collating sequence containing all the 49 characters; instead it contains three partial sequences, expressed as follows:

A is less than B is less than C.... is less than Y is less than Z;

0 is less than 1 is less than 2.... is less than 8 is less than 9;

blank is less than 0, and blank is less than A.

Thus we see that there is no rule about the ordering of the numerals with respect to the letters, nor about the ordering of any of the special characters, apart from that of blank with respect to each of the two partial sequences. On any given computer system there will be a complete collating sequence, but no program should ever make use of any ordering beyond that stated above.

3. Source Form

FORTRAN was developed in the heyday of the punched card and one of the hangovers in the language, which is particularly irritating in the day of the computer terminal, is the rigid source form which the language imposes on the statements of which it is composed.

Each statement consists of one or more *lines*, and each line is usually divided into four *fields* (see Fig. 3), although the standard itself defines only the first three.

Column : 1 — 5   6,   7 ——————— 72   73 ——— 80

     Label   Continuation   Statement   Comment
            Mark

Fig. 3 The FORTRAN source form

The first field contains, where applicable, a *statement label,* used to identify certain types of statement. The label must be numeric, containing from one to five digits, one of which must be non-zero. Any embedded blanks are ignored. For reasons of readability, it is customary, but not obligatory, to position labels to the right-hand edge in the label field. The values used as labels are often subject to certain conventions; these will be discussed in Chapter 9. The appearance and legibility of a program suffer when too many labels are used, and we shall see later how to reduce their number to as few as possible.

A FORTRAN statement may be written on up to 20 consecutive lines. The first line of a multi-line statement is known as the *initial line* and the succeeding lines as *continuation lines*. A line is an initial line or a continuation line depending on whether there is a character, other than zero or blank, in column 6 of the line, which is the second field. Otherwise the character used to indicate a continuation line is completely arbitrary, but a good practice is to use a meaningful symbol such as + :

```
    X = (− Y + DISCR2)
  +    /2*A
```

Columns 1 to 5 of continuation lines must be blank.

The third field, from columns 7 to 72, is reserved for the FORTRAN statements themselves. Within the statements, blank characters have no meaning or significance (with one exception which we shall meet in Section 2.5 below). This allows us to use blanks freely to improve the appearance of the statements, for instance by placing all equals signs between blanks in order to draw a clear distinction between the left- and right-hand sides of assignments.

The fourth field, from columns 73 to 80, has no significance and may be used for short comments, line sequence numbers or similar applications.

4. Comment Lines

It is usually quite difficult to understand a section of program code, merely by reading the code itself. The code may contain mathematical expressions whose origin and purpose are not obvious, and the program logic may well be complex, depending on the algorithms employed. To help with understanding, both by the author and by others, FORTRAN allows the code to be interspersed with *comment lines*. These lines have no significance whatsoever for the program, and may contain any sequence of characters allowed by the computer being used. In particular, many computers allow the use of lower-case characters in comment lines. A comment line is distinguished from statements by the presence of an asterisk (*) in column 1 of the line. For compatibility with the previous FORTRAN standard, a character C in column 1 is also accepted as indicating a comment line, but the new form should always be used, in order to identify positively a program as conforming to the latest standard, for example

   * This is a comment line.

A line which is completely blank in columns 1 to 72 is also regarded as a comment line.

A comment line may appear anywhere in a program, except after the END statement of the final program unit.

The sensible use of comment lines in program units will be the subject of Chapter 12.

5. Constants

The FORTRAN language allows us to define various constants for use in calculations or in other types of expressions. There are six types of constant, corresponding to the six data types defined by the language. The first type is the *integer constant* which is simply a signed or unsigned integer value consisting of a sequence of digits:

   1
   0
   -999
   32767
   $+10$

The *range* of the integers is not specified in the language, but on a computer with a word size of n bits, is often from $-2^{(n-1)}$ to $+2^{(n-1)}-1$. Thus on a $16-$ bit computer the range is from -32768 to $+32767$ (see also Section 7.2).

The second type of constant is the *real constant* which is a floating-point form built of some or all of: a signed or unsigned integer part, a decimal point, a fractional part, a signed or unsigned exponent part. One or both of the integer part and fractional part must be present. An exponent part consists of the letter E followed by a signed or unsigned integer. One or both of the decimal point and the exponent part must be present. An example is

$$-10.6E-11 \text{ meaning } -10.6 \times 10^{-11}$$

and other legal forms are

$$1. \quad -0.1 \quad 1E-1 \quad 12.3456789$$

Once again, neither the range of the exponent nor the allowed number of significant digits is specified by the standard. Common values are about 10^{-79} to 10^{+79} for the range, with a limit on significance of about six decimal digits.

To overcome the problem of insufficient significance, and hence accuracy, in many mathematical calculations, especially on computers with a 32-bit word size or less, the third constant type, the *double-precision constant,* is available. This has a similar form to that of the real constant, except that the exponent must always be present, and specified with a D. Examples are

$$1.D1 \quad -1.D-3 \quad 2D4$$

FORTRAN, as a language widely used for numerical and engineering calculations, has the advantage of having as fourth constant type the *complex constant*. This is designated by a pair of constants, which are either integer or real, separated by a comma and enclosed in parentheses. Examples are

$$(1., 3.2) \qquad\qquad (1, .99E-2)$$

where the first constant of each pair is the real part of the complex number, and the second constant is the imaginary part. The range and significance of each part are identical to those of the real constants.

The fifth type of constant is the *logical constant* which has one

of two values, either .TRUE. or .FALSE.. These logical constants
are normally used only to initialize logical variables to their required
values, as we shall see in the next chapter.

The final type of constant is the *character constant* which consists of a string of arbitrary length of any characters enclosed in
apostrophes:

'ANYTHING GOES'

The apostrophes serve as delimiters, and are not part of the value
of the constant. The value of the constant

'STRING'

is

STRING

We note that in character constants the blank character becomes significant, (this is the exception noted above):

'A STRING'

is not the same as

'ASTRING'

A problem arises with the representation of an apostrophe itself
in a character constant. In this case, any embedded apostrophe is
simply doubled, without an intervening blank:

'ISN''T IT A NICE DAY'

and to express a single apostrophe, ', as a character constant, we
then write

''''

6. Symbolic Names

A FORTRAN program references many different entities, such as
variables, named constants, program units, external files and storage
areas. The names by which these entities are referenced are known

as *symbolic names,* and according to the FORTRAN syntax must consist of between one and six alphanumeric characters (*i.e.* either letters or numerals), of which the first must be a letter. There are no other restrictions on the names, in particular there are no reserved words in FORTRAN. We thus see that valid names are, for example

A
ATHING
X1
MASS
Q123
REAL
THE NUT

and invalid names are

1A	First character not alphabetic
VARIABLE	Too long
$SIGN	Contains non-alphanumeric character
GO!	Contains illegal character
CHARACTER	Too long
01234Z	First character not alphabetic

Within the constraints of the syntax, it is important to choose names which have a clear significance − these are known as *mnemonic names.* Examples are DAY, MONTH and YEAR, for variables to store the calendar date, as opposed to names such as D, M and Y, or worse still A, Q and R1 for the same purpose.

7. Variables

We have seen in the section on constants that there exist six different data types. To each of these six types there corresponds a variable type. These may be divided into two classes: in the first are the integer and real variables, and in the second are the double-precision, complex, logical and character variables. The two classes differ in that integer and real variables do not necessarily require an explicit *declarative statement* which indicates their type. Any variable whose name begins with I, J, K, L, M or N is an integer variable, unless otherwise declared, and any variable whose name begins with any other letter, *i.e.* A to H or O to Z, is similarly a real variable unless otherwise declared.

The simplest way by which a variable may be declared to be of a particular type is by specifying its name in a type declaration such as

```
INTEGER I
REAL A
DOUBLE PRECISION EXACT
COMPLEX CURRNT
LOGICAL PRAVDA
CHARACTER LETTER
```

These declaration statements will be met again in Section 5.2. Suffice it to state here that it can be a very confusing practice to override the default typing of integer and real variables, and it is normally better to choose variable names corresponding to the default type. Thus, the use of a variable named AMASS is preferable to a declaration

```
REAL MASS
```

The range and significance of the variables are the same as those of the corresponding constants, described in Section 2.5. The main difference is with character variables, for which the length of the variable must be specified if it is different from one. In the example above, the variable LETTER has the default length of one, and may, therefore, have the value of any single character, but not more. To declare a variable called WORD intended to hold a word up to a maximum of 20 characters in length, we would need a declaration

```
CHARACTER*20 WORD
```

8. Arrays

When programming, it is often useful to be able to manipulate objects which are more sophisticated than simple variables. Compound objects of more than one variable are called *data structures* and the principal data structure supported by FORTRAN is the *array*. (In Chapter 6 we shall meet the COMMON block, which is also a data structure). An array consists of an ordered set of elements, all of the same data type. There are a number of ways in which arrays may be declared; for the moment we will consider only the declaration of arrays of real elements. To declare an array named A of 10 real elements, we use the statement

REAL A(10)

which will reserve 10 logically consecutive memory locations. The first element of the vector is A(1) and the last A(10).

Many problems require a more elaborate declaration than one in which the first element of a vector is designated 1, and it is possible in FORTRAN to declare a lower as well as an upper bound:

REAL VECTOR($-10:5$)

This is a vector of 16 elements, the first being VECTOR(-10) and the last VECTOR(5). We thus see that whereas we always need to specify the upper bound of an array, the lower bound is optional, and by default 1.

An array may extend in more than one dimension, and FORTRAN allows up to seven dimensions to be specified:

REAL B(5,4)

declares an array with two dimensions, and

REAL GRID($-10:5$, $-20:-1$, 0:1, $-1:0$, 2, 2, 2)

declares seven dimensions, the first four with explicit lower bounds. It may be seen that the size of this second array is 16x20x2x2x2x2x2 = 10240, and that arrays of many dimensions can place large demands on the memory of a computer.

The ordering of the elements in an array is such that successive elements of a column are in contiguous memory locations. Thus the first element of GRID is GRID($-10, -20, 0, -1, 1, 1, 1$) and this is followed by GRID ($-9, -20, 0, -1, 1, 1, 1$). The last element is GRID($5, -1, 1, 0, 2, 2, 2$). This is illustrated for an array of two dimensions in Fig. 4. (This shows incidentally that the row and column storage convention is the opposite to the addressing convention used in matrix algebra).

To reference an element of an array we specify, as in the examples above, each element by its *subscript* values. In the examples we used integer constants, but in general each subscript may be formed of an *integer expression,* that is, any arithmetic expression whose value is of type integer. The subscript must always be in the ranges

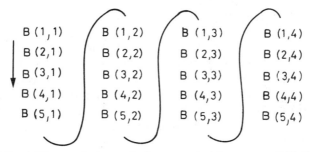

$$\begin{array}{cccc} B(1,1) & B(1,2) & B(1,3) & B(1,4) \\ B(2,1) & B(2,2) & B(2,3) & B(2,4) \\ B(3,1) & B(3,2) & B(3,3) & B(3,4) \\ B(4,1) & B(4,2) & B(4,3) & B(4,4) \\ B(5,1) & B(5,2) & B(5,3) & B(5,4) \end{array}$$

Fig.4 The ordering of elements in the array B(5,4)

defined in the array declaration and there must be as many subscripts as dimensions. Examples are

    A(1)
    A(I*J)
    A(NINT(X + 3.))
    A(IPOINT(I + 1))

where NINT is a standard function to convert a real value to the nearest integer (see Appendix A), and IPOINT is an array of indices, pointing to array elements. (From the last example we notice that FORTRAN, unlike some other programming languages, has no pointer data type, and pointers must be programmed explicitly.)

9. Character Substrings

It is possible to build arrays of characters, just as it is possible to build arrays of any other variables:

    CHARACTER LINE(80)

declares an array, called LINE, of 80 elements, each one character in length. Each character may be addressed by the usual reference, LINE(I) for example. In this case, however, a more appropriate declaration might be

    CHARACTER*80 LINE

which declares a single variable of 80 characters. These may be referenced individually or in groups using a *substring* notation

    LINE(I:J)

LINE(I:J)

which references all the characters from I to J in LINE. Here we have used the colon to separate the two substring subscripts. The colon is obligatory in substring references, and so to reference a single character we require LINE(I:I). There are default values for the substring subscripts. If the lower one is omitted the value 1 is assumed, if the upper one is omitted, a value corresponding to the length of the variable is assumed. Thus,

LINE(:I)	is equivalent to LINE(1:I)
LINE(I:)	is equivalent to LINE(I:80)
LINE(:)	is equivalent to LINE or LINE(1:80)

We may now combine the length declaration with the array declaration to build arrays of character variables of specified length, as in

CHARACTER*80 PAGE(60)

which might be used to define storage for the characters of a whole page, with 60 elements of an array, each of length 80. To reference the line J on a page we may write PAGE(J), and to reference the Ith character on that line we could combine the array subscript and character substring notations into

PAGE(J)(I:I)

At this point we must note a number of limitations associated with character variables. Firstly, there is no defined mapping of characters onto computer words, and so the number of characters stored in a word varies from computer to computer. Thus, in order to avoid problems when transferring programs between computers, the character data type is subject to certain restrictions which we shall meet in later chapters. Secondly, it is not possible to define a null or empty character string. Thirdly, as we have seen, character variables are of a pre-defined maximum fixed length, making it impossible to manipulate variables of variable length. Nevertheless, even with these restrictions, this data type is adequate for most character manipulation applications.

10. Summary

In this chapter we have introduced the elements of the FORTRAN language. The character set has been listed, and the manner in which its components may be combined to form constants and variables explained. In this context we have encountered the six data types defined in FORTRAN, and seen how each data type has corresponding constants and variables. The variables may be used in the construction of one of FORTRAN's data structures, the array, and we have introduced one method by which arrays may be declared, and also seen how their elements may be referenced by subscript expressions. The concept of the substring has been presented for character variables and arrays. In the following chapter we shall see how these elements may be combined into expressions and statements, FORTRAN's equivalents of 'phrases' and 'sentences'.

Exercises

1. For each of the following assertions, state whether it is true, false or not determined, according to the FORTRAN collating sequences:

    B is less than M
    8 is less than 2
    * is greater than T
    $ is less than /
    blank is greater than A
    blank is less than 6

2. Which of the FORTRAN lines in Fig. 5 are correctly written according to the requirements of the FORTRAN source form? Which ones are comment lines? Which lines are initial lines and which are continuation lines?

3. Classify the following constants according to the six data types of FORTRAN. Which are not legal constants?

− 43	'WORD'
4.39	1.9 − 4
0.0001E + 20	'STUFF AND NONSENSE'
4 9	(0.,1.)
(1.D3,2)	'I CAN''T'
'(4.3E9, 6.2)'	4D9
E5	'SHOULDN' 'T'

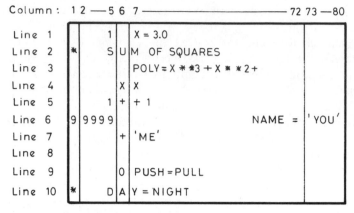

Fig. 5 FORTRAN source lines

4. Which of the following names are legal FORTRAN names?

NAME   NAME32
QUOTIENT   123
A182C3   NO – GO
STOP!   BURN

5. Given the type declarations

INTEGER HIGH
LOGICAL FLAG
REAL I

what are the types of the following variables?

LOW   I
FLAG1   HIGH
I10   REAL

6. What are the first, tenth, eleventh and last elements of the following arrays?

REAL A(11)
REAL B(0:11)
REAL C(– 11:0)
REAL D(10,10)
REAL E(5,9)
REAL F(5,0:1,4)

7. Given the array declaration

CHARACTER*10 C(0:5,3)

which of the following element substring references are legal?

C(2,3)	C(4:3)(2,1)
C(6,2)	C(0,0)
C(0,3)	C(2,1)(4:8)
C(4,3)(:)	C(3,2)(0:9)
C(5)(2:3)	C(5:6)
C(5,3)(9)	C(,)

3 EXPRESSIONS AND ASSIGNMENTS

1. Introduction

We have seen in the previous chapter how we are able to build the 'words' of FORTRAN – the constants, variables and other names – from the basic elements of the character set. In this chapter we shall discover how these entities may be further combined into 'phrases' or *expressions,* and how these, in turn, may be combined into 'sentences', or *assignment statements.*

In an expression we express a sequence of computations which is to be carried out by the computer. The result of the computation is then assigned to a named variable or array element. A sequence of assignments is the way in which we specify, step-by-step, the series of individual computations to be carried out, in order to arrive at the desired result. There are three separate sets of rules for expressions and assignments, depending on whether the variables in question are arithmetic, logical or character in type, and we shall discuss each set of rules in turn, before turning to the relational expressions which we need in order to understand the next chapter on control statements.

An expression in FORTRAN is formed of operands and operators, combined in a way which follows the rules of FORTRAN syntax. The simplest expression has the form

$$operand \ operator \ operand$$

an example being

$$X + Y$$

There are two cases, which we shall meet below, of a unary operator in expressions of the form

operator operand

The operands are either constants, variables, array elements or functions (see Chapter 6).

The result of a simple expression may itself be used as an operand, and in this way we can build up more complicated expressions:

operand *operator* operand *operator* operand

where consecutive operands are separated by a single operator.

The rules of FORTRAN state that the components of expressions are evaluated successively from left to right for operators of equal precedence (once again with an exception to be met below). If it is necessary to evaluate part of an expression, or *sub-expression*, before another, parentheses may be used to indicate which sub-expression should be evaluated first. In

operand *operator*(operand *operator* operand)

the sub-expression in parentheses will be evaluated first, and the result used as an operand to the first operator.

2. Arithmetic Expressions

An *arithmetic expression* is an expression whose operands are one of the four arithmetic types — integer, real, double-precision and complex — and whose operators are

**	exponentiation
* /	multiplication, division
+ −	addition, subtraction

The operators are listed here in their order of precedence. In the absence of parentheses, exponentiations will be carried out before multiplications and divisions, and these before additions and subtractions.

We note that the minus sign (−) can be used as a unary operator, as in

$$-\text{TAX}$$

(throughout this book the default typing of variables is assumed, unless otherwise stated).

The exception to the left-to-right rule noted above concerns exponentiations. Whereas the expression

$$A + B + C$$

will be evaluated from left to right as

$$(A + B) + C$$

the expression

$$A**B**C$$

will be evaluated as

$$A**(B**C)$$

Of note is the difference between the two expressions

$$-1.**I$$

which always evaluates to $-1.$, and

$$(-1.)**I$$

which evaluates to $-1.$ for odd values of I, and to 1. for even values of I.

For the data types real, double-precision and complex, computations will be carried out to the precision available on a given computer, but for integer data types the results of any division will be truncated to the integer value whose magnitude is equal to or less than the magnitude of the exact result. Thus, the result of

6/3	is 2
8/3	is 2
$-8/3$	is -2

This fact must always be borne in mind whenever arithmetic expressions involving integer divisions are written.

The rules of FORTRAN allow an arithmetic expression to contain arithmetic operands of differing types. This is known as a *mixed-mode expression.* Under these rules, the weaker of the two data types (the one with less precision or using fewer storage units) will be converted, or *coerced,* into the type of the stronger one. The result will also be that of the stronger type. If, for example, we write

A*I

then I will be converted to a real data type before the multiplication is performed, and the result of the computation will also be of type real. The rules are summarized for each possible combination for the operations +, −, * and / in Table 2, and for the operation ** in Table 3. In both Tables, I stands for integer, R for real, DP for double precision and C for complex.

Table 2

Type of result of a.op.b, where .op. is +, −,* or /

Type of a	Type of b	Value of a used	Value of b used	Data type of result
I	I	a	b	I
I	R	REAL(a)	b	R
I	DP	DBLE(a)	b	DP
I	C	CMPLX(REAL(a),0.)	b	C
R	I	a	REAL(b)	R
R	R	a	b	R
R	DP	DBLE(a)	b	DP
R	C	CMPLX(a,0.)	b	C
DP	I	a	DBLE(b)	DP
DP	R	a	DBLE(b)	DP
DP	DP	a	b	DP
DP	C	−	−	Prohibited
C	I	a	CMPLX(REAL(b),0.)	C
C	R	a	CMPLX(b,0.)	C
C	DP	−	−	Prohibited
C	C	a	b	C

Table 3

Type of result of a**b

Type of a	Type of b	Value of a used	Value of b used	Data type of result
I	I	a	b	I
I	R	REAL(a)	b	R
I	DP	DBLE(a)	b	DP
I	C	CMPLX(REAL(a),0.)	b	C
R	I	a	b	R
R	R	a	b	R
R	DP	DBLE(a)	b	DP
R	C	CMPLX(a,0.)	b	C
DP	I	a	b	DP
DP	R	a	DBLE(b)	DP
DP	DP	a	b	DP
DP	C	–	–	Prohibited
C	I	a	b	C
C	R	a	CMPLX(b,0.)	C
C	DP	–	–	Prohibited
C	C	a	b	C

3. Arithmetic Assignment

An analogous set of rules applies during an assignment. The general form of an arithmetic assignment is

$$var = exp$$

where *var* is an arithmetic variable name or array element, and *exp* is any arithmetic expression. If *exp* is not of the same type as *var*, it will be converted to that type before the assignment is carried out. Here we note that if the type of *var* is integer but *exp* is not, then the assignment will result in a loss of precision due to a truncation. Similarly, if a double-precision expression is assigned to a real variable, a loss of precision will occur. Thus, the values in I and A following the assignments

$$I = 7.3$$
$$A = 4.01934867D0$$

are 7 and 4.01935, respectively (assuming a computer with six decimal digits of precision). Similarly, the assignment of a complex quantity to a non-complex variable involves the loss of the imaginary part.

4. Logical Expressions and Assignments

Logical constants, variables, array elements and functions may appear as operands in logical expressions. The logical operators, in decreasing order of precedence, are

.NOT.	logical negation
.AND.	logical intersection
.OR.	logical union
.EQV. and .NEQV.	logical equivalence and non-equivalence

If we assume a logical declaration of the form

LOGICAL I,J,K,L

then the following are valid logical expressions:

.NOT. J
J .AND. K
I .OR. L .AND. .NOT. J
(.NOT. K .AND. J .NEQV. .NOT. L) .OR. I

In the first expression we note the use of .NOT. as a unary operator. This is the second example of a unary operator which we noted above. In the third expression, the rules of precedence imply that the sub-expression L.AND..NOT.J will be evaluated first, and the result OR'ed with I. In the last expression, the two sub-expressions .NOT.K.AND.J and .NOT.L will be evaluated and compared for non-equivalence. The result of the comparison, .TRUE. or .FALSE., will be OR'ed with I.

We note that the .OR. operator is an inclusive operator; there is no exclusive OR in FORTRAN, *i.e.* one that evaluates to .FALSE. if both operands are .TRUE..

The result of any logical expression is the value .TRUE. or .FALSE., and this value may then be assigned to a logical variable or to the element of a logical array (FLAG in this example):

FLAG(3) = (.NOT. K .EQV. L) .OR. J

A logical variable or array element may be set to a predetermined value by an assignment statement:

FLAG(1) = .TRUE.
FLAG(2) = .FALSE.

In the foregoing examples all the operands and results were of type logical – no other data type is allowed to participate in a logical operation or assignment.

5. Character Expressions and Assignments

The only operator allowed in character expressions is the concatenation operator //. This has the effect of combining two character operands into a single character result, *i.e.* the result of concatenating the two character constants 'AB' and 'CD', written as

'AB'//'CD'

is the character string ABCD. The operands may be character variables, array elements, substrings or functions. For instance, if WORD1 and WORD2 are both of length 4, and contain the character strings LOOP and HOLE respectively, the result of

WORD1(4:4)//WORD2(2:4)

is the string POLE.
    The length of the result of a concatenation is the sum of the lengths of the operands. Thus, the length of the result of

WORD1//WORD2//'S'

is 9, *i.e.* the length of the string   LOOPHOLES .
    The result of a character expression may be assigned to a character variable, array element or substring. Assuming the declarations

CHARACTER*4 CHAR1, CHAR2
CHARACTER*8 RESULT

we may write

```
CHAR1 = 'ANY '
CHAR2 = 'BOOK'
RESULT = CHAR1//CHAR2
```

In this case RESULT will now contain the string ANY BOOK. We note in these examples that the lengths of the left- and right-hand sides of the three assignments are in each case equal. If, however, the length of the result of the right-hand side is shorter than the length of the left-hand side, then the result is placed in the leftmost part of the left-hand side and the rest is filled with blank characters. Thus, in

```
CHARACTERS*5 FILL
FILL(1:4) = 'AB'
```

FILL(1:4) will have the value ABbb (where b stands for a blank character). The value of FILL(5:5) remains undefined, that is, it contains no specific value and should not be used in an expression. On the other hand, when the left-hand side is shorter than the result of the the right-hand side, the right-hand end of the result is truncated. The result of

```
CHARACTER*5 TRUNC8
TRUNC8 = 'TRUNCATE'
```

is to place in TRUNC8 the character string TRUNC.

Care has to be taken when manipulating substrings taken from the same variable or array, as no part of the left-hand and right-hand sides of an assignment may overlap. Thus, the assignment

```
RESULT(1:3) = RESULT(3:5)
```

is illegal. Where subscript expressions are used, such errors may be more difficult to identify, as in

```
RESULT(I:J) = RESULT(K:L)
```

which may or may not be legal, depending on the possible values of the subscripts.

6. Relational Expressions

It is possible in FORTRAN to test whether one expression bears a certain relation to another. The relational operators are

.LT.	less than
.LE.	less than or equal
.EQ.	equal
.NE.	not equal
.GT.	greater than
.GE.	greater than or equal

The result of such a comparison is one of the values .TRUE. or .FALSE., and we shall see in the next chapter how such tests are of great importance in controlling the flow of a program. Examples of relational expressions are

I .LT. 0	integer relational expression
A .LT. B	real relational expression
A + B .GT. I − J	mixed mode relational expression
CHAR1 .EQ. 'Z'	character relational expression
	(assuming CHAR1 is type character)

All the data types except logical may participate in a relational expression.

In the third expression above, we note that the two components are of different arithmetic types. In this case, and whenever the two components consist of expressions which require evaluation, the rules state that the components are to be evaluated separately, and the final test made on the difference of the two results. Thus, a relational expression such as

A + B .LE. I − J

will be evaluated as though it had been written

((A + B) − (I − J)) .LE. 0.

involving, of course, a conversion of the result of (I − J) to type real.

We note the precedence of the arithmetic operators over the relational operators.

As stated above, the result of a relational expression is either

.TRUE. or .FALSE., and this value may be assigned to a logical variable or array element:

LOGICAL COND
:
COND = A .GT. B

Similarly, the results of several relational expressions may be combined into a logical expression, and assigned, as in

COND = A .GT. B .OR. X .LT. 0. .AND. Y .GT. 1.

where we note the precedence of the relational operators over the logical operators.

7. Summary

In this chapter we have seen how the different kinds of expressions – arithmetic, logical and character – may be formed, and how the corresponding assignments of the results may be made. The relational expressions have also been presented. We now have the information required to write short sections of code forming a sequence of statements to be performed one after the other. In the following chapter we shall see how more complicated sequences, involving branching and iteration, may be built up.

Exercises

1. Which of the following are valid arithmetic expressions?

A + B	− C
A + − C	D + (− F)
(A + C)**(P + Q)	(A + C)(P + Q)
− (X + Y)**I	(4.*((A − D) − (A + 4.*X)) + 1)

2. In the following expressions, add the parentheses which correspond to FORTRAN's rules of precedence (assuming I − N are type logical): *e.g.*

A + B**2/C   becomes   A + ((B**2)/C)

C + 4.*F
4.*G − A + B/2.
A**B**C**D

A*B – C**D/A + B
I .AND. J .OR. K
.NOT. L .OR   .NOT. I .AND. M .NEQV. N

3. What are the results of the following expressions?

3 + 4/2	6/4/2
3.*4**2	3.**3/2
– 1.**2	(– 1.)**3

4. A character variable R has length 8. What are the contents of R after each of the following assignments?

```
R  =  'ABCDEFGH'
R  =  'ABCD'//'01234'
R(:7)  =  'ABCDEFGH'
R(:6)  =  'ABCD'
```

5. Which of the following relational expressions are valid?

B .LE. C	P .LT. T .GT. O.
X – 1 .GT. Y	X + Y .LT. 3 .OR. .GT. 4.
B.LT.C.AND.3.0	Q.EQ.R .AND. S.GT.T

6. Write expressions to compute:

a) the perimeter of a square of side L;

b) the area of a triangle of base B and height H;

c) the volume of a sphere of radius R.

7. An item costs n cents. Write assignment statements which compute the change to be given from a $1 bill for any value of n from 1 to 99, using coins of denomination 1, 5, 10 and 25 cents.

4 CONTROL STATEMENTS

1. Introduction

We have learnt in the previous chapter how assignment statements
may be written, and how these may be ordered one after the other
to form a sequence of code which is executed step-by-step. In most
computations, however, this simple sequence of statements is by
itself inadequate for the formulation of the problem. For instance,
we may wish to follow one of two possible paths through a section
of code, depending on whether a calculated value is positive or negative. We may wish to sum all the 1000 elements of an array, and
to do this by writing 1000 additions and assignments is clearly tedious; the ability to iterate over a single addition is required instead.
We may wish to pass control from one part of a program to
another, or even stop processing altogether.

For all these purposes we have available in FORTRAN various
facilities to enable the logical flow through the program statements
to be controlled. The facilities contained in standard FORTRAN do
not correspond to those now widely regarded as being the most
appropriate for a modern programming language, and it is then even
more important that the ones that are available to us are used in a
selective and careful way. This will be explained at the relevant
points in the course of this chapter.

2. Branches

In this section we shall consider one of the most disputed statements
in programming languages – the GO TO in its various guises. It is
generally accepted that it is difficult to understand a program which
is interrupted by many branches, especially if there is a large

number of backward branches − those returning control to a statement preceding the branch itself. Excessive use of backward and forward branches leads to what is known as a 'spaghetti' style of programming, which is recognized to be difficult to test and nearly impossible to modify. At the same time there are certain occasions, especially when dealing with error conditions, when GO TO statements are required in even the most advanced languages. In FORTRAN, they must be used even for normal program control, but a sign of a good FORTRAN program style is nevertheless a simple logic flow characterized by few branches.

2.1 Unconditional GO TO

The simplest form of branch instruction is the unconditional GO TO, which has the form

GO TO *sl*

where *sl* is a statement label. This statement label must be present on an executable statement in the same program unit (a statement which can be executed, as opposed to one of an informative nature, like a declaration). An example is

```
    X = Y + 3.
    GO TO 4
    :
  3 X = X + 2.
  4 Z = X + Y
```

in which we note that after execution of the first statement, a branch is taken to the last statement, labelled 4. The statement labelled 3 is jumped over, and can be executed only if there is a branch to the label 3 somewhere else in the program unit. If the statement following an unconditional GO TO is unlabelled it can never be reached and executed, creating *dead code,* normally a sign of incorrect coding.

2.2 Computed GO TO

The second form of branch statement is the computed GO TO, which enables one path among many to be selected, depending on the value of an integer expression. The general form is

GO TO *(sl1, sl2, sl3,...)* [,] *intexp*

where *sl1, sl2, sl3 etc.* are statement labels, which must appear in the same program unit, and *intexp* is any integer expression. The final comma is optional. This is indicated by the square brackets which are not part of the statement, a convention used throughout the book. An example is

GO TO (6,10,20) $I(K)**2 + J$

which references three statement labels. When the statement is executed, then if the value of the integer expression is 1, the first branch will be taken, *i.e.* control is transferred to the statement labelled 6. If the value is 2, the second branch will be taken, and so on. If the value is less than 1, or greater than 3, no branch will be taken, and the next statement following the GO TO will be executed.

This type of statement is most useful when deciding between a number of different alternatives which can be selected on the basis of an integer expression which evaluates to values in the range 1 to *n,* where *n* is the number of labels in the statement. For instance, if a program is dealing with data which can be of six different categories, each of which is distinguished by a keyword KEY which has a value between 1 and 100 for one category type, between 101 and 200 for another, and so on, then we may write

GO TO (1,2,3,4,5,6) $(KEY - 1)/100 + 1$

*

*   Handle out of range value of KEY

and any invalid value of KEY will be handled by the following statements.

2.3 Assigned GO TO

The final form of branch statement is actually written in two parts, an ASSIGN statement and an assigned GO TO statement. The form is

ASSIGN *sl1* TO *intvar*

:

ASSIGN *sl2* TO *intvar*

:

GO TO *intvar [[,] (sl1, sl2, ...)]*

where *sl1, sl2 etc.* are statement labels, and *intvar* an integer
variable. When an ASSIGN statement is executed, *intvar* acquires the
value of a statement label. Different labels may be assigned in different parts of the program unit. When the assigned GO TO is executed, then depending on the final value of *intvar*, the appropriate
path is taken. The optional statement label list in the GO TO statement should, if present, contain a list of all the valid values of *intvar*, and permits a check that it has acquired an expected value during program execution.

   The assigned GO TO is a little-used statement, whose main purpose is to control logic flow in a program unit having a number of
paths which come together at one point at which some common
code is executed, and from which a new branch is taken depending
on the path taken before. This is shown in Ex. 1, where we see
three paths joining before the GO TO, and three after.

```
      :
      X  =  Y + 1.
      ASSIGN 4 TO JUMP
      GO TO 3
    1 X  =  Y + 2.
      ASSIGN 5 TO JUMP
      GO TO 3
    2 X  =  Y + 3
      ASSIGN 6 TO JUMP
    3 Z  =  X**2
      :
      GO TO JUMP (4,5,6)
      :
```

Example 1

   The variable JUMP in the example may be defined only in an
ASSIGN statement, and may not appear, for instance, on the
left-hand side of a normal assignment statement.

3. IF Statements

The IF statements provide a mechanism for branching depending on
a condition. There are three types of IF statement, known as the
arithmetic IF, the logical IF and the block IF. The first of these has
become almost a relic, and is little used. The other two are powerful
tools, the block IF being a generalized form of the logical IF which,

when used properly, greatly facilitates the writing and reading of code.

3.1 Arithmetic IF

The arithmetic IF provides a three-way branching mechanism, depending on whether an arithmetic expression has a value which is less than, equal to, or greater than zero. Its general form is

IF *(exp) sl1, sl2, sl3*

where *exp* is any valid arithmetic expression, and *sl1, sl2* and *sl3* are the labels of statements in the same program unit. If the result obtained by evaluating *exp* is negative then the branch to *sl1* is taken, if the result is zero the branch to *sl2*, and if the result is greater than zero the branch to *sl3*. An example is

```
    IF (P − Q) 1,2,3
  1 P  =  0.
    GO TO 4
  2 P  =  1.
    Q  =  1.
    GO TO 4
  3 Q  =  0.
  4 ...
```

in which a branch to 1, 2 or 3 is taken depending on the value of P − Q. The arithmetic IF may be used as a two-way branch when two of the labels are identical:

IF (X − Y) 1,2,1

but the logical IF, to be described next, is to be preferred in this case, as it is easier to understand. As there are few genuine three-way branches in most programs, and as experience shows that the arithmetic IF is often incorrectly coded, its use should be kept to an absolute minimum.

3.2 Logical IF

In the case of the logical IF, the value of a logical expression is tested, and a single statement executed if its value is .TRUE. . If the value is .FALSE. then the next statement is executed. The general form is

IF *(lexp) st*

where *lexp* is any logical expression, and *st* is any statement except another logical IF, any of the statements associated with the block IF (such as an ELSE), the beginning of a DO-loop, or an END statement (these are all described later in this chapter). Examples are

```
IF (FLAG) GO TO 6
IF (X − Y .GT. 0.) X = 0.
IF (COND .OR. P.LT.Q .AND. R.LE.1.) S(I,J) = T(J,I)
```

The logical IF is normally used either to perform a single assignment depending on a condition, or to branch depending on a condition, and is to be preferred to the arithmetic IF for this second purpose. Compare

```
IF (I − J) 2,2,1
1 Y = 0.
2 .......
```

with

```
IF (I.GT.J) Y = 0.
```

In the second version the test is explicitly stated, and there are no statement labels.

3.3 Block IF

The block IF allows either the execution of a sequence of statements to depend on a condition, or the execution of alternative sequences of statements to depend on alternative conditions. The simplest of its three forms is

```
IF (lexp) THEN
   sts
ENDIF
```

where *lexp* is any logical expression and *sts* is any sequence of executable statements (except an END statement or an incomplete DO-loop, which we shall meet in the next section). We notice that the block IF is a compound statement, the beginning being marked by the IF...THEN, and the end by the ENDIF. An example is

```
IF (X.LT.Y) THEN
   TEMP = X
   X = Y
   Y = TEMP
ENDIF
```

in which we notice also that the body of the IF block is indented with respect to its beginning and end. This is not obligatory, but makes the logic easier to understand, especially in nested IF blocks as we shall see below.

In the second form of the block IF, an alternative sequence of statements is executable, for the case where the condition is .FALSE. . The general form is

```
IF (lexp) THEN
   sts1
ELSE
   sts2
ENDIF
```

in which the first sequence of statements (sts1) is executed if the condition is .TRUE. and the second sequence (sts2), following the ELSE statement, is executed if the condition is .FALSE. . The ELSE statement and the following statements associated with it are known as an ELSE *clause*. An example is shown in

```
IF (X.LT.Y) THEN
   X = -X
ELSE
   Y = -Y
ENDIF
```

in which the sign of X is changed if X is less than Y, and the sign of Y is changed if X is greater than or equal to Y.

The third and most general type of block IF uses the ELSEIF statement to make a series of independent tests, each of which has its associated sequence of statements. The tests are made one after the other until one is fulfilled, and the associated statements of the ELSEIF clause are executed. Control then passes to the end of the IF block. If no test is fulfilled, no statements are executed, unless there is a final 'catch-all' ELSE clause. The general form is seen in Ex. 2. There can be an arbitrarily high number of ELSEIF statements, and zero or one ELSE statements.

```
IF (I.EQ.1) THEN
   J = K
ELSEIF (I.EQ.2) THEN
   J = L
ELSEIF (I.EQ.3) THEN
   J = M
ELSE
   J = 0
ENDIF
```

Example 2

The statements within an IF block may be labelled, but the labels must never be referenced in such a fashion as to pass control into the range of an IF block or ELSE clause or ELSEIF clause from outside the range of the respective block or clause. The range is defined as the sequence of statements between the beginning of the block or clause and the next ELSEIF, ELSE or ENDIF statement, whichever comes first. Thus the following sequence is illegal:

```
   GO TO 1        < − −illegal branch
   :
   IF (TEMP.GT.100.) THEN
      BOIL = .TRUE.
      STEAM = .TRUE.
   ELSE
1     BOIL = .FALSE.
      LIQUID = .TRUE.
   ENDIF
```

Block IF's may be nested within one another to an arbitrary depth, as shown to two levels in Ex. 3, in which we see again the necessity to indent the code in order to be able to understand the logic easily.

Nested block IFs are one of the most powerful facilities of FORTRAN, enabling one to write clear code with very few branches and hence few statement labels, and consequently fewer possibilities for making errors.

```
IF (I.LT.0) THEN
   IF (J.LT.0) THEN
      X = 0.
      Y = 0.
   ELSE
      Z = 0.
   ENDIF
ELSEIF (K.LT.0) THEN
   Z = 1.
ELSE
   X = 1.
   Y = 1.
ENDIF
```

Example 3

4. DO-loops

Many problems in mathematics require for their representation in a programming language the ability to *iterate*. If we wish to sum the elements of an array A of length 10, we could write

```
SUM  =  A(1)
SUM  =  SUM + A(2)
:
SUM  =  SUM + A(10)
```

which is clearly laborious. FORTRAN provides a facility known as the DO-loop which allows us to reduce these ten lines of code to

```
SUM  =  0.
DO 1 I  =  1,10
   SUM  =  SUM + A(I)
1 CONTINUE
```

In this fragment of code we first set SUM to zero, and then require that the statements between the DO statement and the statement labelled 1, inclusive, shall be executed ten times. For each iteration there is an associated value of an index, kept in I, which assumes the value 1 for the first iteration through the loop, 2 for the second, and so on up to 10. I is a normal variable, but is subject to the rule that it may not be explicitly modified within the DO-loop. The CONTINUE statement is a 'do-nothing' operation.

The CONTINUE statement in a DO-loop is not obligatory, and in fact a DO-loop may terminate on any executable statement except an unconditional or assigned GO TO, an arithmetic IF or any statement associated with a block IF, a RETURN, STOP, END or another DO statement. However, the use of a CONTINUE to mark the termination of a DO-loop is recommended in order to provide a clear definition of its end, just as indentation of the body of the loop is recommended to highlight the control flow.

The DO statement in our example above has more general forms. If we wished to sum the fourth to ninth elements we would write

    DO 1 I = 4,9

thereby specifying the required first and last values of I. If, alternatively, we wished to sum all the odd elements, we would write

    DO 1 I = 1,9,2

where the third of the three loop *parameters,* namely the 2, specifies that I is to be incremented in steps of 2, rather than by the default value of 1, which is assumed if no third parameter is given. In fact, we can go further still, as the parameters need not be constants at all, but expressions, as in

    DO 1 I = J + 4, M, − K(J)**2

in which the first value of I is J + 4, and subsequent values are decremented by K(J)**2 until the value of M is reached. DO-loops may thus run 'backwards' as well as 'forwards'. If any of the three parameters is a variable, its value may be modified within the loop without affecting the number of iterations, as the *initial* values of the parameters are used for the control of the loop.

So far, only integer values and expressions have been shown, but the completely general form of the DO statement is

    DO *sl [,] var = exp1, exp2 [,exp3]*

where *var* is an integer, real or double-precision variable, and *exp1, exp2* and *exp3* (which is optional and non-zero) are any valid integer, real or double-precision expressions. We may therefore write a loop such as

DO 1 A = 1, 15.7, 2.1

in which A will assume the initial value of 1.0 (note the conversion), and will subsequently have the values 3.1, 5.2, *etc.* up to 15.7.

There are, however, serious problems associated with DO-loops with non-integer parameters or indices, but in order to understand them we first need to define how the number of iterations of a DO-loop is actually determined. The standard states that this number is given by

$$\text{MAX(INT}((exp2 - exp1 + exp3)/exp3), 0)$$

where INT is a function we shall meet later (in Chapter 6) which converts an arithmetic expression to an integer value (if necessary) according to the conversion rules we have learnt during the discussion of assignments (in Section 3.3). MAX is a function which, in this case, returns either this value or zero, whichever is the larger. There are two consequences following from this definition, the first predictable, the second not necessarily predictable. If a loop begins with the statement

DO 1 I = 1,N

then its body will not be executed at all if the value of N on entering the loop is zero or less. This is an example of the *zero-trip loop,* and is the consequence of the application of the MAX function.

The second consequence is more insidious, and results from the application of the INT function. Consider the statement

DO 1 A = -0.3, -2.1, -0.3

which we would normally expect to result in seven iterations of the loop it controls. The number of iterations is obtained from the result of a computation whose intermediate value may not be 7.00000.. but 6.99999.., due to rounding errors. After applying the INT function we then have the integer 6 as the number of iterations. Whether or not this rounding error will occur for a given loop on a given computer is difficult to foresee, and this is the reason for avoiding the use of floating-point DO-loop parameters.

A similar problem is associated with the use of a floating-point loop index in conjunction with floating-point loop parameters, and results from the fact that the new index value for each iteration is obtained by adding the value of the third loop parameter (or unity if it is absent) to the loop index used in the foregoing iteration. For integer values this is perfect: in the sequence of statements I = I + 1 implied by

DO 1 I = 10,100

nothing can go wrong. However, in the sequence A = A + 0.000001 implied by

DO 1 A = 10., 100., 0.000001

catastrophes can occur, as the result of adding 0.000001 to 10 is not necessarily 10.000001, and repeating 90000001 times the same type of operation will lead to a very peculiar final value of A. Since this type of error can be hidden in the results of expressions whose values are unknown when writing the code, we have another reason for avoiding the use of floating-point parameters.

We have just seen how the value of a DO-loop index is incremented at the end of every loop iteration for use in the subsequent iteration. As the value of the index is available outside the loop after its execution, we have three possible situations, each illustrated by the following loop:

```
DO 1 I = 1,N
    :
    :
    IF (I.EQ.J) GO TO 2
    :
    :
1 CONTINUE
2 L = I
```

If, at execution time, N has the value zero or less, I is set to 1 but the loop is not executed, and control passes to the statement labelled 2, the first to follow the termination of the loop. The value assigned to I, and hence to L, is 1.

If, on the other hand, N has a value which is greater than or equal to J, an exit will be taken at the IF statement, and L will acquire the last value of I, which is of course J.

If, as a third possibility, the value of N is greater than zero but less than J, the loop will be executed N times, with the successive values of I being 1, 2,... *etc.* up to N. When reaching the end of the loop for the N*th* time, I will be incremented a final time, acquiring the value $N+1$, which will then be assigned to L. We see how important it is to make careful use of loop indices outside the range of their loops, especially when there is the possibility of the number of iterations taking on one of the boundary values, zero or the maximum for the loop.

The range of a DO-loop, just mentioned, is the sequence of statements following the DO statement and including the statement bearing the statement label specified in the DO statement. It is prohibited to jump into the range of a DO-loop from anywhere outside its range. The following sequence is thus illegal:

```
    GO TO 2                          < − −illegal branch
    :
    DO 1 I = 1,10
    :
 2    A = B+C
    :
 1 CONTINUE
```

It is similarly illegal for the ranges of a DO-loop and an IF block (or ELSEIF or ELSE clause) to be only partially contained in one another. A DO-loop must be completely contained in a block or clause, or the IF block completely contained in the DO-loop. The following two sequences are thus legal:

```
    IF (lexp) THEN
        DO 1 I = 1,10
        :
 1      CONTINUE
    ELSE
        :
    ENDIF
```

and

```
    DO 1 I = 1,10
        IF (lexp) THEN
        :
        ENDIF
 1 CONTINUE
```

but this third sequence is not:

```
      IF (lexp) THEN
         DO 1 I = 1,10
         :
      ENDIF    < - -illegal position of IF block termination
    1 CONTINUE
```

DO-loops may be nested within themselves, following a similar rule that the range of one loop must be completely contained within the range of another. We may thus write a matrix multiplication as

```
      DO 1 I = 1,N
         DO 1 J = 1,M
         A(I,J) = 0.
            DO 1 L = 1,K
            A(I,J) = A(I,J)+B(I,L)*C(L,J)
    1 CONTINUE
```

In this example, the two loops share the same terminal statement; in general this is not the case, as in

```
      DO 1 I = 1,N
         SUM = 0.
         DO 2 J = 1,I
            SUM = SUM+B(J,I)
    2    CONTINUE
         A(I) = SUM
    1 CONTINUE
```

and, indeed, code is easier to modify if each loop has its own separate termination.

5. Summary

In this chapter we have introduced the three main features by which the control in FORTRAN code may be programmed − the GO TO statements, the IF statements and the DO-loop. The effective use of these features is the key to sound code.

There are four further statements which are used to control the flow of a program, but as they are used principally to control the flow between program units rather than within a program unit, we will leave their discussion until we reach that topic in Chapter 6. However, in order to be able to write and test short, whole

```
*
*       Print a conversion table of the Farenheit
*        and Celsius temperature scales
*       between specified limits.
*
        CHARACTER SCALE
*
*       Read SCALE and limits
      1 READ *, SCALE, LOWTMP, IHITMP
*
*       Check for valid data
        IF (SCALE.NE.'C' .AND. SCALE.NE.'F') GO TO 3
*
*       Loop over the limits
        DO 2 ITEMP = LOWTMP, IHITMP
*
*       Choose conversion formula
           IF (SCALE.EQ.'C') THEN
              CELST = ITEMP
              FARHT = 9./5.*CELST + 32.
           ELSEIF (SCALE.EQ.'F') THEN
              FARHT = ITEMP
              CELST = 5./9.*(FARHT-32.)
           ENDIF
*
*       Print table
        PRINT*, CELST, ' DEGREES C CORRESPOND TO'
      +     ,FARHT, ' DEGREES F'
      2 CONTINUE
        GO TO 1
*
*       Termination
      3 PRINT *, 'END OF VALID DATA'
        END


'C'  90  100
'F'  20   32
'*'   0    0
```

Example 4

programs we need to introduce the END, READ and PRINT statements.

We have touched several times upon the concept of a *program unit* as being like the chapter of a book. Just as a book may have just one chapter, so a complete program may consist of just one program unit, which is known as a *main program.* In its simplest form it consists of a series of statements of the kinds we have been dealing with so far, and terminates with an END statement, which acts as a signal to the computer to stop processing the current program.

In order to test whether a program unit of this type works correctly, we need to be able to output, to a terminal or printer, the values of the computed quantities. This topic will be fully explained in Chapter 7, and for the moment we need to know only that this can be achieved by a statement of the form

    PRINT * , ' VAR1 = ', VAR1 , ' VAR2 = ', VAR2

which will output a line such as

    VAR1 = 1.0 VAR2 = 2.0

Similarly, input data can be read by statements like

    READ *, VAL1, VAL2

This is sufficient to allow us to write simple programs like that in Ex. 4, which outputs the converted values of a temperature scale between specified limits. Valid inputs are shown at the end of the example.

Exercises

1. Write a program which

    a) defines an array to have 100 elements;
    b) assigns to the elements the values 1,2,3,....100;
    c) reads two integer values in the range 1 to 100;
    d) reverses the order of the elements of the array in the range specified by the two values.

2. The first two terms of the Fibonacci series are both 1, and all subsequent terms are defined as the sum of the preceding two terms.

Write a program which reads an integer value LIMIT and which computes and prints the first LIMIT terms of the series.

3. The coefficients of successive orders of the binomial expansion are shown in the normal Pascal triangle form as

$$
\begin{array}{ccccccccc}
 & & & & 1 & & & & \\
 & & & 1 & & 1 & & & \\
 & & 1 & & 2 & & 1 & & \\
 & 1 & & 3 & & 3 & & 1 & \\
1 & & 4 & & 6 & & 4 & & 1
\end{array}
$$

etc.

Write a program which reads an integer value LIMIT and prints the first LIMIT lines of this Pascal triangle.

4. Define a character variable of length 80. Write a program which reads a value for this variable. Assuming that each character in the variable is alphabetic, write code which sorts them into alphabetic order, and prints out the frequency of occurrence of each letter.

5. Write a program to read an integer value LIMIT and print the first LIMIT prime numbers, by any method.

5　SPECIFICATION STATEMENTS

1. Introduction

In the preceding chapters we have learnt firstly the elements of the FORTRAN language, then how they may be combined into expressions and assignments, and finally how we may control the logic flow of a program unit by branching and iterating. We have seen that this knowledge is sufficient to write short programs, when combined with a rudimentary PRINT statement and with the END statement. Already in Chapter 2, we met some declaration or *specification statements* when dealing with the logical, double-precision, complex and character data types; unless otherwise specified, variables are assigned default types, integer or real, according to their initial letter. In this chapter we shall examine some more of FORTRAN'S specification statements, stressing those which are useful in writing code of a high standard from the point of view of style, and deprecating those which are harmful in this respect.

To begin with, however, it is necessary to recall the place of specification statements in a programming language. A program is processed by a computer in (usually) three stages. In the first stage, *compilation*, the *source code* (text) of the program is read and processed by a program known as a *compiler* which analyses it, and generates a file containing *object code*. Each program unit of the complete program is processed separately. The object code is a translation of the source code into a form which can be understood by the computer hardware, and contains the precise *instructions* as to what operations the computer is to perform. In the second stage of processing, the object code is placed in the relevant part of the computer's storage system by a program often known as a *loader* which prepares it for the third stage. During this second stage, the separate program units are linked to one another, *i.e.* joined to form a complete executable program. The third stage consists of the *execution*, whereby the coded instructions are performed and the results of the computations made available.

During the first stage, the compiler requires information about the constants, variables, arrays and other entities which it cannot deduce from the executable statements themselves. This information is provided, mainly at the beginning of each program unit, by the specification statements, whose description is the subject of this chapter.

2. Type Statements

There is a controversy in the world of computing about an issue know as *strong typing*. Many modern programming languages require that the type of each variable, array or other data structure or language entity be defined explicitly. Any variable encountered in an executable statement and whose type has not been declared, will cause the compiler to indicate an error in the code. In the case of FORTRAN, type definitions are required for only four of the six data types. Any variable appearing in the code and which is not explicitly typed will be assigned to type real or integer, depending on its initial letter (see Section 2.7). This absence of strong typing can lead to program errors if a variable name, for instance, is misspelt, in which case the misspelt name will be a separate variable of type real or integer. There is no completely certain method of writing specification statements in a way which avoids this weakness, but they will be introduced here in a manner which leads at least to a compromise.

To declare any variable, array or other entity as being of a specific type we can use statements of the form

type nlist

where *type* is one of INTEGER, REAL, DOUBLE PRECISION, COMPLEX, LOGICAL or CHARACTER, and *nlist* is a list of variable names, array names and, as we shall see in the next chapter, function names. Examples are

```
INTEGER LAST, LONG(100), MESH(0:10, 0:10)
REAL TEMP(0:100)
DOUBLE PRECISION FINE(50, 10)
COMPLEX Q1(20), Q2(20)
```

```
LOGICAL FLAG(-10:10)
CHARACTER*8 WORD(4), POINT*1, TEXT(20)*4
```

There are two important points to notice in these declarations. The first is that all arrays are declared directly with their dimensions. This is not strictly necessary, as we shall see below, but is a way of ensuring that all arrays are assigned an explicit type along with their dimensions, and increases the probability of a compiler detecting a misspelt name in the array declarations. If, for instance, FLAG had been misspelt as FLOG, any reference to an element of FLAG in a logical expression would lead to a compile-time error, as it would appear to be real because of the default type assignment.

The second point is the length specifications in the CHARACTER statement. The first length specification, immediately following the keyword CHARACTER, is an optional asterisk and value which assign a default length to each character entity appearing in the statement. If no such length is specified, this default value is assumed to be one. It is possible to override this default specification by assigning a specified length to any given entity, as is shown for POINT and TEXT in the example; the name of the entity is followed by an asterisk and the length required. The length can be either an unsigned integer constant, as shown above, or an *integer constant expression* enclosed in parentheses (see next Section), or an asterisk enclosed in parentheses (Section 6.3.1).

The default typing of real and integer values can be changed using the IMPLICIT statement, which also allows a default typing for the other data types to be specified. For instance, to make all the entities in a program unit type INTEGER, we use

```
IMPLICIT INTEGER (A-Z)
```

which states that all entities whose name starts with a letter from A to Z, *i.e. all* entities, shall be of default type INTEGER. The general form is illustrated by

```
        IMPLICIT LOGICAL (L), CHARACTER*4 (C),
    +           REAL (A-B,D-K,M-Z)
```

which specifies that all entities whose initial letter is L are of type LOGICAL, all whose initial letter is C are CHARACTER and length 4, and all others (A, B, D to K and M to Z) are REAL.

The implicit typing specified in such statements may be further overridden by explicit type statements following any implicit ones:

```
IMPLICIT REAL (A – Z)
INTEGER IPOINT, FIRST, LAST
```

means that all entities will be of type REAL, except for the three named variables IPOINT, FIRST and LAST, which are of type INTEGER.

The effect of strong typing can almost be achieved by making a global implicit typing to a little-used data type, such as LOGICAL or CHARACTER, depending on the program in question. The implicit typing is followed by explicit type declarations for all the entities used in the program unit, as in

```
IMPLICIT LOGICAL (A – Z)
REAL nlist
INTEGER nlist
```

If, in the executable statements, any variable name is misspelt, it will be assumed to be of the LOGICAL data type, and when used in an expression will give a compile-time error. For example, in

```
IMPLICIT LOGICAL (A – Z)
REAL AXE, GRIND
AX = 0.
GRIND = 1.
```

the first assignment statement is illegal, and will be reported as such by a compiler, because a real value cannot be assigned to a logical variable.

3. PARAMETER Statement

Inside a program unit, we often need to define a constant or set of constants. For instance, in a program requiring repeated use of the speed of light, we might define among the first executable statements

```
C = 2.9979251
```

and use the variable C in the subsequent expressions. A danger in this practice is that somewhere later the value of C may be over-written inadvertently, for instance because another programmer re-uses C as a variable to contain a different quantity, failing to notice that the name is already in use.

Another situation which can arise is that the program contains specifications such as

    REAL X(10), Y(10), Z(10)
    INTEGER MESH(10, 10), IPOINT(100)

where all the dimensions are 10 or 10**2. Such specifications may be used extensively, and 10 may even appear as an explicit constant, say as a parameter in a DO-loop which processes these arrays:

    DO 1 I = 1,10

Later it may be realised that the value 20 rather than 10 is required, and the new value must be substituted laboriously everywhere the old one occurs, an error-prone and tedious undertaking.

In order to deal with both of these situations, FORTRAN contains what are known as *symbolic constants*. These are named constants which are defined in PARAMETER statements, and which may never appear on the left-hand side of an assignment statement. They may be used in any way in which a usual constant may be used. Thus we may write

    PARAMETER (C = 2.9979251)

and the value is protected, as C is now a *symbolic name* and may not be used as a variable name in the same program unit. Similarly, we may write

    PARAMETER (LENGTH = 10)
    REAL X(LENGTH), Y(LENGTH), Z(LENGTH)
    INTEGER MESH(LENGTH, LENGTH), IPOINT(LENGTH**2)
    :
    DO 1 I = 1, LENGTH

which has the clear advantage that in order to change the value of 10 to 20 only a single line must be modified, and the new value is then correctly propagated throughout the program unit.

In the example above, the expression LENGTH**2 appeared in one of the dimension specifications. This is a particular example of the general case, which allows any integer constant expression to be used in a dimension specification. *i.e.* any expression containing integer constants or symbolic constants, such as

    LENGTH + 20/LENGTH

In the definition of a symbolic constant we may use any constant expression, *i.e.* any expression using constants or symbolic constants but not involving an exponentiation to a real power, *e.g.*

PARAMETER (LSQ = LENGTH**2, PI = 355./113.)

Note in this example that it is possible in one statement to define several symbolic constants, in this case two, separated by commas.

Any symbolic constant used in the definition of another symbolic constant must appear in a PARAMETER statement positioned before such use, or to the left of its use in the same PARAMETER statement. Similarly, if the type of a symbolic constant is specified in an IMPLICIT statement, that statement must appear before the PARAMETER statement concerned:

IMPLICIT INTEGER (A, P)
PARAMETER (APPLE = 3, PEAR = APPLE**2)

Finally, there is an important point concerning the definition of a character symbolic constant. The appearance of a symbolic name in a PARAMETER statement is sufficient to define also its length, which does not have to be specified separately in the corresponding CHARACTER specification statement. The fact that the length will be specified later is indicated by a dummy length specification signified by (*), and this obviates the need to count the length of such character strings, and makes modifications to their definitions much easier. An example of this is

CHARACTER STRING*(*)
PARAMETER (STRING = 'NO NEED TO COUNT')

The PARAMETER statement is an important means whereby constants may be protected from overwriting, and programs modified in a safe way. It should be used for these purposes on every possible occasion. Note, however, that symbolic constants cannot be used in the definition of a constant, for instance as the real or imaginary part of a complex constant.

4. DIMENSION Statement

We have seen how we may specify the dimensions of an array when declaring its type:

    REAL A(0:10, 0:10)

There is an alternative method of declaring array dimensions without
using a type statement. This is achieved using the DIMENSION
statement, as shown in the following example:

    CHARACTER*8 C
    DIMENSION A(10), I(10), C(10)

This statement declares A and I to be arrays of length 10 and of
default type real and integer, respectively. The array C is also of
length 10, its type and element length being declared in a separate
type declaration.

    The DIMENSION statement is a convenient means of declaring
the dimensions of arrays of different types in a single statement, but
in practice it is safer to use type statements with their explicit typing
for this purpose.

    The DIMENSION statement may, of course, be combined with
the PARAMETER statement:

PARAMETER (LENGTH = 20)
DIMENSION IPOINT(LENGTH), BUFFER(LENGTH, LENGTH)

and to the extent that it is used at all, should always be based on
symbolic constants for other than trivial declarations.

5. EQUIVALENCE Statement

Another statement whose use should be kept to a strict minimum is
the EQUIVALENCE statement, which is a means whereby a given
storage area may be referenced by two or more different names. For
instance, it may be that a program unit has been written using a
variable name AA. It is later realised that a better name for AA
would have been ANGLE, and this changeover can be partly
achieved by the statement

    EQUIVALENCE (AA, ANGLE)

which allows AA and ANGLE to be used interchangeably in the
program text, as both names now refer to the same storage location.
In other words, it is immaterial whether we write

    AA = 3.

or

ANGLE = 3.

as both assignments have the same effect, changing the same designated location. (It is far better, of course, to perform a global edit of the code, if this facility is available on the computer being used).

Another application of the EQUIVALENCE statement is to give variable names to array elements, as in

REAL A(3)
EQUIVALENCE (ALPHA, A(1)), (BETA, A(2)), (GAMMA, A(3))

which names each element of the array A, allowing the variable names ALPHA, BETA, GAMMA, to be used instead of the elements of A: A(1), A(2), A(3), respectively. This example also shows how more than one equivalence may be defined in one statement, separated by commas.

It is possible to equivalence arrays together. In

REAL A(3,3), B(3,3), COL1(3), COL2(3), COL3(3)
EQUIVALENCE (COL1, A, B), (COL2, A(1,2)), (COL3, A(1,3))

the two arrays A and B are equivalenced, and each column of A (and hence of B) is equivalenced to an array COL1, *etc.* We note in this example that when an array is referenced without a subscript the whole array is intended, and also that more than two entities may be equivalenced together, even in a single declaration.

Lastly, it is possible to equivalence variables of different types, except that CHARACTER variables may be equivalenced only with variables of the same type as in

CHARACTER A*4, B(2)*3
EQUIVALENCE (A, B(1)(3:))

where the character variable A is equivalenced to the last four characters of the six characters of the character array B. Another example for different types is

INTEGER I(100)
REAL X(100)
EQUIVALENCE (I, X)

where the arrays I and X are equivalenced. This might be used, for instance, to save storage space if I is used in one part of a program unit and X separately in another part. This is a highly dangerous practice, as considerable confusion can arise when one storage area contains variables of two or more data types, and program changes may be made very difficult if the two uses of the one area are to be kept distinct. There may even be an inadvertent interference between the two uses, leading to program errors. The problem can be compounded if the two data types concerned occupy a different number of storage units (see Section 7.2) as is the case when, for instance, real variables are equivalenced with double-precision variables.

In the subscript and substring expressions shown so far, explicit constants have been employed. It is equally possible to use any integer constant expression, as in

```
PARAMETER (JOIN = 10)
REAL A(10*JOIN), B(100*JOIN)
EQUIVALENCE (A(JOIN), B(10*JOIN + 100))
```

What is clearly not possible, is for an entity to appear in equivalence statements in such a way that it is assigned to two different storage locations. Nor can array elements or character substrings appear in a way which would cause their order in storage to be modified. Thus in

```
REAL A(2), B(2), C
EQUIVALENCE (C, A(1)), (C,A(2))
EQUIVALENCE (A(1), B(2)), (A(2), B(1))
```

both EQUIVALENCE statements are illegal for the reasons stated.

The EQUIVALENCE statement was once of great use in reducing the storage requirements of programs, as it allows large arrays to share the same locations in a controlled fashion. Now that computer storage is relatively cheap, this need no longer exists. On the contrary, the dangers of storage association are so great that the EQUIVALENCE statement should be used for that purpose only *in extremis*.

It was often customary to write complicated equivalence statements in which several arrays were overlapped with one another, perhaps combined with equivalenced variable names for some of the array elements. This practice led to code which was difficult to understand, and well-nigh impossible to modify correctly. In modern programs, the EQUIVALENCE statement should be avoided as far as possible, even at the cost of increased space, as clear code is nowadays usually a more important consideration.

6. DATA Statement

When introducing the PARAMETER statement, a distinction was drawn between the initialization of constants and of variables. For the former the PARAMETER statement should be used; for the latter an initial assignment is possible. For variables and arrays, however, another possibility for initialization exists, namely the DATA statement. This statement has certain advantages which will become clearer in the next chapter; for the moment its application within a single program unit will be described.

The form of the DATA statement is

DATA *nlist/clist/*[[,] *nlist/clist/*]...

where *nlist* is a list of variable, array, array element or substring names and *clist* is a list of initial values. A simple example is

DATA A, B, C/1., 2., 3./, I, J, K/1, 2, 3/

in which the variable A acquires the initial value 1., B the value 2., *etc.* These values are initialized once only by the compiler, and *not* each time the program unit containing the DATA statement is executed. There must be as many constants in each *clist* as elements in each *nlist*.

Constants which repeat may be written once and combined with a *repeat count* which may be a symbolic constant as well as an explicit, integer constant:

DATA I,J,K/3*0/

Arrays may be initialized in three different ways: by name, by element or by an *implied* DO-loop. These three ways are shown below for an array declared by

REAL A(5,5)

Firstly, for the whole array, the statement

DATA A/25*1.0/

sets each element of A to 1.0. Since repeat counts can group several constants, a statement like

DATA A/5*(1.,2.,3.,4.,5.)/

could be used to initialize the array A with a repeating pattern of constants.

Secondly, individual elements of A may be initialized, as in

DATA A(1,1), A(3,1), A(1,2), A(3,3)/2*1.0, 2*2.0/

in which four specified elements only are initialized.

When the elements to be selected fall into a pattern which can be represented by DO-loop indices, it is possible to write DATA statements a third way, like

DATA (A(I,1), I=1,5,2) /3*0./

or

PARAMETER (L=5, ONE=1.0, NINE=((L+1)/2)**2)
DATA ((A(J,I), I=1,J), J=1,L,2)/NINE*ONE/

This second example sets to 1.0 the first element of the first row of A, the first three elements of the third row, and all the elements of the last row, as shown in Fig. 6. In a nested DO-loop of this kind, the loop in the innermost pair of parentheses is taken first, and then the next, and so on until the outermost loop is reached.

```
1.0       .       .       .       .

 .        .       .       .       .
1.0      1.0     1.0      .       .

 .        .       .       .       .
1.0      1.0     1.0     1.0     1.0
```

Fig. 6 Result of an implied DO-loop in a DATA statement

Subscript and substring expressions in DATA statements may be any integer constant expression, as shown by

CHARACTER*80 STRING
PARAMETER (I1=24, I2=29)
DATA STRING(I1+4: I2−1)/'X'/

where the usual assignment rules apply if the constant is not of the same length as the variable.

In the examples given so far, the types of the constants in a *clist* have always been the same as the type of the entities in the corresponding *nlist*. This need not always be the case. When an entity in the *nlist* is of an arithmetic type, integer, real, double-precision or complex, the corresponding constant may be of *any* of these four types. If the two types differ, the entity is initialized following the rules for mixed-mode assignments given in Section 3.3. It is thus permissible to write statements such as

DATA Q/1/, I/3.1/, B/(0.,1.)/, C/1.D3/

(where the types are all default). One of the few uses of this possibility is to initialize a single-precision variable to a double-precision constant, as in

DATA PI/3.141592653D0/

on a machine with adequate precision, say a 36-bit word size or more. When moving a program containing such constants to a machine with inadequate precision, it is sufficient to add the statement

DOUBLE PRECISION PI

to maintain the precision of the constant. Normally, of course, such fundamental constants should be set in a PARAMETER statement, where a similar mixed-mode definition is possible.

In the next chapter we shall elaborate on the allowed positions of specification statements in a program unit. Normally they appear before any of the executable statements, but the DATA statement is an exception to this rule: although it must be placed after all other specification statements, it may appear *anywhere* after those statements, even being mixed in with the executable statements. Good programming practice, however, requires that DATA statements be grouped together immediately after the other specification statements. Placing them amongst the executable statements gives an untidy appearance to the code, and makes the DATA statements themselves less apparent.

7. Summary

In this chapter some of the specification statements of FORTRAN have been introduced. There are some others, but as they are concerned more with the way that a whole program is built out of program units, they will be dealt with more appropriately in the next chapter.

Of the statements described above, the type, PARAMETER, IMPLICIT and DATA statements all find their proper place in well written code. Of the other two, the DIMENSION and EQUIVALENCE statements, the former is not really needed at all, and the latter is required only in some special cases. Both should be used sparingly, resulting in code which is more likely to be free of errors than would otherwise be the case.

Exercises

1. Write suitable type statements for the following quantities:

    i) an array to hold the number of counts in each of the 100 bins of a histogram numbered from 1 to 100.

    ii) an array to hold the temperature at points equally spaced at 1cm intervals on a rectangular grid 20cm square, with points in each corner.

    iii) an array to describe the state of 20 on/off switches.

    iv) an array to contain the information destined for a printed page of 44 lines each of 70 letters or digits.

2. Explain the difference between the following pairs of declarations:

       PARAMETER (I = 3.1)
       IMPLICIT REAL (I)

and

       IMPLICIT REAL (I)
       PARAMETER (I = 3.1)

What is the value of I in each case?

3. Write type and DATA statements to initialize:

i) all the elements of an integer array of length 100 to the value zero.

ii) all the odd elements of the same array to 0 and the even elements to 1.

iii) the diagonal elements of a real 10x10 square array to 1.0 .

iv) a character string to the digits 0 to 9.

6 PROGRAM UNITS

1. Introduction

In the previous chapters we have dealt with the various components from which it is possible to build individual program units. In this chapter we shall consider the various types of program units (or procedures) which are defined in FORTRAN, and discuss how complete programs may be built from them, and how the program units themselves interact with one another and with the data and the data structures that they share.

It is possible in FORTRAN to write a complete program as a single unit, and indeed this was a fairly common practice in the early days of programming. As we shall see in Chapter 10, it is now considered to be preferable to break down the different functions to be performed by a program into manageable units of, say, not more than 100 lines of code. Each unit corresponds to one program task, and can ideally be written and tested in isolation.

A complete program must, as a minimum, include one *main program,* containing specification statements and executable statements. These statements we have met so far in examples. Normally, however, a main program will consist of a series of invocations or *calls* to subsidiary programs known as *subprograms.* These are of two types, *function* subprograms and *subroutine* subprograms, and are usually referred to simply as functions and subroutines. They differ mainly in that a subroutine performs a task, whereas a function returns a value which is determined by its *arguments,* and hence is usually, but not necessarily, a function in the mathematical sense. There is a fourth type of program unit, used solely to initialize variables using DATA statements, known as a *block data* subprogram.

We shall, in this chapter, not only describe each of the four types of program unit, but also complete the description of the specification statements, two of which are concerned with the way data are shared between program units, and two with the specification of subprogram names. These four specification statements are thus more appropriately dealt with here in the context of program units. In addition, the description of three of the control statements will be completed, as these are more relevant to the control of program units than to the control of individual lines, or groups of lines, of executable code.

2. Main Program

A FORTRAN main program consists of four ordered parts (ignoring any comment lines):

  i) an optional header line

  ii) optional specification statements

  iii) one or more executable statements

  iv) an END line

The optional header line consists of a statement of the form

    PROGRAM *pname*

where *pname* is any allowed FORTRAN name, for instance

    PROGRAM PASCAL

Most of the optional specification statements and the executable statements we have met already.

The END line of a main program has two purposes. Firstly it acts as a signal to the compiler that it has reached the end of the program unit, and secondly it is a statement which, when executed, causes the execution of the complete program to stop.

The END statement, although so simple, has a special syntactical rule associated with it: that it must appear as an initial line without continuation lines in the source code. It is possible to label the END statement and branch to it anywhere in the main program, thus stopping the execution of the program:

```
      GOTO 999
      :
999   END
```

Another means of stopping the execution of a program is to execute a STOP statement. This statement may be labelled, or be combined with a logical IF statement, and may appear anywhere in a main program or subprogram. Normally, well designed programs always return control to the main program for program termination, and so the STOP statement should appear only there, if at all. However, in applications where several STOP statements appear in various places in a complete program, it is possible to distinguish which of the STOP statements has caused termination by associating with each one a unique character constant, or a string of up to five digits. This might be used by a given processor to indicate the origin of the STOP in a message. Examples are

```
      STOP
      STOP 12345
      STOP 'INCOMPLETE DATA. PROGRAM TERMINATES'
```

3. Subroutines

A simple program might typically consist of three basic parts – an initialization part, a processing part and an output part. In the first part the initial conditions for the computations are defined, in the second part these computations are performed, and in the third part the results of the computation are output to a terminal, or line printer, or other peripheral device such as a disc. It is most convenient to code such a structure in three distinct procedures, which in FORTRAN are known as *subroutines*. Subroutines are invoked by the CALL statement, as shown in the main program in Ex. 5. A given subprogram must never call itself either directly, or indirectly by calling another subprogram which in turn calls the first subprogram.

In this example we have the main program for a programmed version of a card game, in which each of four subroutines is called in turn, each performing a single logical task. To play a game several times, it would be sufficient to enclose the appropriate calls inside a DO-loop.

However there is something missing from this program – there is no sign of any flow of information between the subroutines. How does PLAY know which cards DEAL has dealt? There are, in fact, two methods by which such information may be passed. The first is

```
        PROGRAM GAME
*
*       MAIN PROGRAM TO CONTROL A GAME OF
*       CARDS
*
*       FIRST THE SHUFFLE CARDS
        CALL SHUFFL
*
*       THEN DEAL THEM
        CALL DEAL
*
*       PLAY THE GAME
        CALL PLAY
*
*       DISPLAY THE RESULT
        CALL RESULT
*
*       FINISH THE GAME
        END
```
Example 5

via arguments in the subroutine calls, the second is by defining a storage data area which is common to the subroutines.

3.1 Subroutine variable and array arguments

Let us suppose in our example that subroutine SHUFFL needs to communicate to DEAL the order of the cards in the deck. We can do this by defining an array in the main program:

```
        INTEGER KARDS(52)
```

which is to contain the integer values 1 to 52 in a random order, where each integer value corresponds to a predefined playing card. For instance, 1 stands for the ace of clubs, 2 for the two of clubs *etc.* up to 52 as king of spades. In order to obtain a shuffled deck of cards we can pass this array to SHUFFL as an *actual argument:*

```
        CALL SHUFFL(KARDS)
```

and expect SHUFFL to fill KARDS with the values 1 to 52 in a random order. To do this, the array is received by SHUFFL as a *dummy argument* defined in the first line of the subroutine:

SUBROUTINE SHUFFL(KARDS)

In the specification statements in SHUFFL, the dummy argument must be further defined as an array, for instance with an array declaration identical to the one in the main program. An outline version of SHUFFL is then shown in Ex. 6.

```
      SUBROUTINE SHUFFL(KARDS)
*
* A ROUTINE TO PLACE THE VALUES 1 TO 52 IN
* KARDS IN RANDOM ORDER
*
      INTEGER KARDS(52)
*
* ALGORITHM TO FILL KARDS
      :
      :
*
* RETURN TO THE CALLING PROGRAM
      END
```

Example 6

We can, of course, imagine a card game in which DEAL is going to deal only three cards to each of four players. In this case it would be a waste of time for SHUFFL to prepare a deck of 52 cards, when we need to know only what the first twelve cards are to be. This can be achieved by requesting SHUFFL to limit itself to a certain number of cards, which for convenience we can define as a symbolic constant, NCARDS. This value can also be transmitted to SHUFFL in a *calling sequence:*

```
      PARAMETER(NCARDS = 3*4)
      :
      CALL SHUFFL(KARDS, NCARDS)
```

Inside SHUFFL we would define the array to be of length NCARDS, and the algorithm to fill KARDS would be contained in a DO-loop with NCARDS iterations:

```
      SUBROUTINE SHUFFL(KARDS, NCARDS)
      :
      INTEGER KARDS(NCARDS)
      :
```

```
      DO 1 ICARD = 1, NCARDS
      :
      KARDS(ICARD) = .....
    1 CONTINUE
```

At this stage we have seen how it is possible to pass an array and a constant between two program units. In general, we can provide as an actual argument any expression and any array. Four other types of actual argument will be explained later. The dummy arguments must agree with the actual arguments in type and number, that is, the types of the individual arguments must correspond, and there must be the same number of actual arguments and dummy arguments. However, the names of the entities do not have to be the same. The call to SHUFFL could have been made as

```
      CALL SHUFFL(3*4, KARDS)
```

and the first lines of the subroutine might be

```
      SUBROUTINE SHUFFL(LIMIT, LIST)
      :
      INTEGER LIST(LIMIT)
```

The important point is that subroutines can be written independently of one another, the association of the dummy arguments to the actual arguments occurring each time the call is executed. We can imagine SHUFFL being used in other programs which use different names, but as long as the agreement of type and number is maintained, SHUFFL will perform its task in exactly the same way. In this manner, libraries of subroutines can be built up.

In our example, the array KARDS has been filled with values by SHUFFL. When an array is passed, the called subroutine may legally change any element of the array. This is not necessarily the case for a scalar argument. The actual argument corresponding to a scalar dummy argument may be any expression. If the expression is a simple variable or array element or character substring, its value may legally be changed by the called subroutine. If, however, the expression is one which is a constant, a symbolic constant or an expression which has to be evaluated, then the corresponding dummy argument must *never* appear on the left-hand side of an assignment statement in the called subroutine. Unfortunately, there is no means by which a FORTRAN compiler can check observance of this rule, and to breach it can lead to program errors at execution time which are very difficult to find. It is therefore essential to be very disciplined in writing the code for program calls and subroutine declarations, as no automatic check is normally available.

The array KARDS has been declared in two different ways in the preceding examples, once explicitly as of length 52 and once implicitly as of length NCARDS. This latter case is known as an *adjustable* array declaration, as the declared array length depends on a quantity whose value is known only at execution time. For an array with more than one dimension, or with defined lower bounds, any or all of the dimensions or bounds may be defined in this way:

```
SUBROUTINE SHOW(A, I, J, K)
REAL A(I:10, J, 3, 0:K)
```

The values I, J and K could also be passed by another mechanism, the COMMON block, which we shall meet below (Section 6.4).

It is often inconvenient, when passing an array of one dimension, to have to specify the dimension at all. The dimension may depend, for instance, on a variable which one does not wish to place in an argument list. For this case we use the *assumed size* array declaration as in

```
SUBROUTINE SHOW(Q)
REAL Q(*)
```

in which Q is declared to have an unknown dimension. This asterisk may also be used for the last dimension of multi-dimensioned arrays:

```
INTEGER I(3, 6, *)
```

An example is a generalized subroutine to copy the elements of one array to another, as in Ex. 7. We note that assumed size arrays may not appear in I/O lists (Section 7.2.2).

In the case of character arrays, the length of the elements may be declared to be unknown in a similar fashion;

```
SUBROUTINE XYZ(C)
CHARACTER*(*) C(*)
```

declares C to be an assumed size character array whose element length will be transmitted implicitly in the call to the subroutine. This length may be determined explicitly using the LEN function (Appendix A). In this case, C may not appear as an operand in an

```
        SUBROUTINE COPY(A, B, N)
*
*       To copy N elements of A to B
*
        REAL A(*), B(*)
*
        DO 1 I = 1, N
           A(I) = B(I)
      1 CONTINUE
        END
```

Example 7

expression involving a concatenation operation.

Two further points must be mentioned concerning the passing of arguments. Firstly, we have seen in Section 5.5 how variables and arrays may be equivalenced. However, no entity appearing in a list of dummy arguments may also appear in an EQUIVALENCE statement in the same program unit. An equivalenced entity may, of course, be passed as an actual argument to a called program unit.

The second point concerns the passing of an array of one size or number of dimensions, to a dummy argument which is of another size or number of dimensions. It is, for instance, perfectly legitimate to pass just part of a singly-dimensioned array between subroutines, as shown in Ex. 8.

```
        REAL A(100)
        :
        CALL SUB (A(52), 49)
        :
        SUBROUTINE SUB(B,N)
        :
        REAL B(N)
        :
```

Example 8

Here only the last 49 elements of A are available to SUB, as the first array element of A which is passd to SUB is A(52). Within SUB, this element is referenced as B(1).

In the same example, it would also be perfectly legitimate for the declaration of B to be written as

```
        REAL B(7, 7)
```

and for the last 49 elements of A to be addressed as though they were ordered as a 7x7 array. The converse is also true. An array dimensioned 10x10 in a calling subroutine may be dimensioned as a singly-dimensioned array of 100 in the called subroutine. Within SUB, it is illegal to address B(50) in any way, as that would be beyond the declared length of A in the calling routine. (There is unfortunately usually no mechanism by which such illegal addressing can be detected).

These various possibilities for passing parts of arrays, or making changes in their shapes (that is, the number of declared dimensions and the extent in each one), offer a powerful tool for building generalized subroutine libraries, but should always be used with care.

A similar restriction on address ranges exists when passing a character substring as an actual argument. In

```
    CALL CHASUB(WORD(3:4))
```

the called subprogram will receive a character string of length two. No other part of the character variable may be referenced in the called subprogram.

3.2 The END and RETURN statements

We have seen earlier in this chapter that in a main program the END statement has two purposes, one to signal the end of the program unit to the compiler, and the other to stop the execution of the program. In a subroutine, the first purpose is identical. When, however, an END statement is executed in a subroutine it does not stop the program, but passes control from the subroutine to the statement following its call in the calling program unit. Thus, in our card playing example, when the END statement of SHUFFL is executed, control is passed back to the main program, which then calls DEAL. Control can be passed back from any point within a called subroutine by labelling the END and branching to that label:

```
    GO TO 999
    :
999 END
```

Another method of achieving the same effect is to execute a RETURN statement anywhere in the executable code.

3.3 Alternate RETURN

When calling certain types of subroutines, it is possible that specific exceptional conditions will arise, which should cause a break in the normal control flow. It is possible in FORTRAN to anticipate such conditions, and to code different flow paths following a subroutine call, depending on whether the called subroutine has terminated normally, or has detected an exceptional or abnormal condition. This is achieved using the alternate RETURN facility which uses the argument list in the following manner. Let us suppose that the subroutine DEAL receives in an argument list the number of cards in the shuffled deck, the number of players and the number of cards to be dealt to each hand. In the interests of generality, it would be a reasonable precaution for the first executable statement of DEAL to be a check that there is at least one player and that there are, in fact, enough cards to satisfy each player's requirement. If there are no players or insufficient cards, it can signal this to the main program which should then take the appropriate action. This may be written in outline as

```
    1 CALL DEAL(NSHUFF, NPLAY, NHAND, KARDS, *2, *3)
      CALL PLAY
*
      :
*   HANDLE EXCEPTIONS
    2 ........
      :
      GO TO 1
    3 .........
      :
      GO TO 1
```

If the cards can be dealt, normal control is returned, and the call to PLAY executed. If an exception occurs, control is passed to the statement labelled 2 or 3, at which point some action must be taken – to stop the game or shuffle more cards. The relevant statement label is defined by placing the statement label preceded by an asterisk as an actual argument in the argument list. An arbitrarily high number of such alternate returns may be specified, and they may appear in any position in the argument list. Since, however, they are normally used to handle exceptions, they are best placed at the end of the list.

In the called routine, the alternate RETURN is taken by

executing a statement of the form

RETURN *intexp*

where *intexp* is any integer expression. The value of this expression
at execution time defines an index to the alternate RETURN to be
taken, according to its position in the argument list. If *intexp* evaluates to 2, the second alternate RETURN will be taken. If *intexp*
evaluates to a value which is less than 1, or greater than the number of alternate RETURNs in the argument list, a normal RETURN
will be taken. Thus, in DEAL, we may write simply

SUBROUTINE DEAL(NS, NP, NH, KARDS, *, *)
:
IF (NP.LE.0) RETURN 1
IF (NS .LT. NP*NH) RETURN 2

The alternate RETURNs are indicated in the dummy arguments by
asterisks, as shown. We note that in the calling routine the statement label must be given explicitly and, in particular, may not be
given as the integer variable associated with the assigned GOTO
statement.

3.4 PAUSE statement

In the early days of computing it was quite usual for a single executing program to have complete control of a computer. At certain
points in the execution of a program it might have been useful to
pause, in order to allow some possible external intervention in the
running conditions to be made, for instance for an operator to activate a peripheral device required by the program. This could be
achieved by executing a PAUSE statement, which has a syntax like
that of the STOP statement, that is, it may be used just like any
other executable statement, and may also contain an associated character constant, or string of up to five digits, *e.g.*

PAUSE 'PLEASE MOUNT THE NEXT DISC PACK'

Execution is resumed by some form of external command, for
instance one given by an operator. This statement is little used in
modern time-sharing computers.

4. COMMON Blocks

In the previous section we saw how two program units are able to communicate by passing variables, character substrings, values of expressions or arrays between them *via* argument lists. In this section we shall meet an alternative method, one which is more attractive when either the number of arguments becomes too large, and hence awkward to handle, or when many program units require access to the same data.

In FORTRAN, it is possible to define areas of storage known as COMMON blocks. They may be either named or unnamed, as shown by the simplified syntax of the COMMON specification statement,

COMMON */[cname]/ vlist*

in which *cname* is an optional name, following the usual naming rules, and *vlist* is a list of variable names or array names. An unnamed COMMON block is known as a *blank* COMMON block. Examples of each are

COMMON /CARDS/ NSHUFF, NPLAY, NHAND, KARDS(52)

and

COMMON // BUFFER(10000)

in which the named COMMON block CARDS defines a data area containing the quantities which are required by the subroutines of our card playing example, and the blank COMMON defines a large data area which might be used by different routines as a buffer area. The // are optional in blank COMMON.

In order for a subroutine to access the variables in the data area, it is sufficient to insert the COMMON definition in each program unit which requires access to one or more of the entities in the list. Thus, the call to DEAL, and the beginning of that subroutine, may be rewritten as shown in Ex. 9.

In this example, we see that identical occurrences of the COMMON block CARDS appear in the main program and in DEAL. In this fashion, the variables NPLAY and NHAND and the array KARDS are made available to the two program units. The variable NSHUFF is shared in a similar fashion between SHUFFL and DEAL (of course, the COMMON block definition must also

```
PROGRAM GAME
COMMON/CARDS/NSHUFF,NPLAY,NHAND,KARDS(52)
:
CALL SHUFFL
NPLAY = 4
NHAND = 3
:
CALL DEAL(*2, *3)
:
2 .....
:
END
SUBROUTINE DEAL(*, *)
COMMON/CARDS/NSHUFF,NPLAY,NHAND,KARDS(52)
:
IF (NPLAY.LE.0) RETURN 1
IF (NSHUFF .LT. NPLAY*NHAND) RETURN 2
:
```

Example 9

appear in SHUFFL.)

The example contains identical variable names in both appearances of the COMMON block. According to the standard, this is not strictly necessary. In fact, the shared data area may be partitioned in quite different ways in different routines, using different variable names, as long as the total length remains the same. It is thus possible for one subroutine to contain a declaration.

```
COMMON /COORDS/ X, Y, Z, I(10)
```

and another to contain a declaration

```
COMMON /COORDS/ I, J, A(11)
```

This means that a reference to I(1) in the first routine is equivalent to a reference to A(2) in the second. This manner of coding is both untidy and dangerous, and every effort should be made to ensure that all declarations of a given COMMON block declaration are identical in every respect. An exception is blank common, whose length may differ in its various references, and for which the longest definition will apply for the complete program.

Another practice to be avoided is to use the full syntax of the COMMON statement, which allows several COMMON blocks to be defined in one statement, and a single COMMON block to be declared in parts. A combined example is

COMMON /PTS/X,Y,Z /MATRIX/A(10,10),B(5,5) /PTS/I,J,K

which is equivalent to

COMMON /PTS/ X, Y, Z, I, J, K
COMMON /MATRIX/ A(10,10), B(5,5)

which is certainly a more understandable declaration of two shared data areas. The only use for the piece-wise declaration of one block is when the limit of 19 continuation lines is otherwise too low.

The COMMON statement may be combined with the other spec-ification statements which we have met, in particular the type, PARAMETER, DIMENSION and EQUIVALENCE statements. Examples are

COMPLEX CURRNT
COMMON /POWER/ CURRNT(10)

for a type declaration;

PARAMETER (LENGTH = 100)
COMMON /BUFFER/ A(LENGTH), I(LENGTH)

for a parameter declaration;

DIMENSION I(100)
COMMON /COORDS/ I

for a DIMENSION declaration; and

REAL A(10)
EQUIVALENCE (A,B)
COMMON /CHANGE/ B(10)

for an EQUIVALENCE statement.

Combining COMMON declarations with type statements is una-voidable for four of the data types, and perfectly acceptable. The combination of PARAMETER and COMMON declarations is even highly recommended, although great care must be taken to ensure that the statements are absolutely identical for each appearance.

(Some computer systems allow sequences of code such as these to be stored in one place, and to be inserted in an identical form in every program unit where they are referenced by means of a special command.)

On the other hand, the practice of using DIMENSION and EQUIVALENCE statements, combined with COMMON declarations, can lead to confusion and errors, as the information about the defined variables is scattered over several statements, which may be widely separated in the code. Programs containing code of this nature become difficult to maintain and modify and so, as far as possible, all the information about the COMMON variables should be contained in the COMMON declaration itself.

Finally, we note that there is a restriction on the mixing of variables of different data types in a single COMMON block: character variables cannot appear in a COMMON block containing variables of any other data type.

5. SAVE Statement

Let us suppose that we wish to count the number of times a subroutine is entered, in order to use the count as an index, or to print out the number of calls. We might write a section of code such as the following

```
      SUBROUTINE ANY(A,B)
      REAL A(*),B(*)
*
*     DEFINE THE INITIAL VALUE OF THE COUNTER
      DATA KOUNT/0/
      :
      KOUNT = KOUNT+1
      PRINT *, ' KOUNT = ', KOUNT
      A(KOUNT) = B(KOUNT)**2
      :
```

In this example, a *local variable*, KOUNT, (a variable used in a single program unit and not defined in a COMMON block) is initialized to zero and used as a counter, and it is assumed that its current value is available each time the subroutine is called. This is not necessarily the case. The standard allows the computer system being used to 'forget' the new value, the variable becoming *undefined* each time control is returned to the calling program unit. In fact, most systems do not take advantage of the standard to spring

surprises like this on unwary users but, in order to avoid the problem altogether, it is as well to ensure that the value is retained from
one call to the next, by means of the SAVE statement. In the
example above, it is sufficient to add, somewhere before the DATA
statement, the line

SAVE KOUNT

to be sure that the value of KOUNT is always retained between
calls, for further use.

```
SUBROUTINE A
:
CALL B
:
CALL C
:
END
SUBROUTINE B
COMMON /INDEX/ I,J,K
:
I = 3
:
END
SUBROUTINE C
COMMON /INDEX/ I,J,K
:
REAL Q(100), P(100)
:
Q(I) = P(I)
:
```

Example 10

A similar situation can arise with the use of COMMON blocks,
illustrated in Ex. 10. This shows two subroutines, B and C, each of
which contains the COMMON block INDEX, and each of which is
called by subroutine A. In this situation, the standard allows all the
values in INDEX to become undefined after each return of control
from B or C back to A. This means that if, as in the example, B
defines a variable I for subsequent use as an index in C, then I
may be undefined when C is called, depending on the computer system used. Once again, this potential hazard can be avoided by
recourse to the SAVE statement. In this case, the statement

        SAVE /INDEX/

has to be inserted in the specification statements of B and C, and
the values of *all* the entities in INDEX will be retained each time
control is passed from either B or C back to A. The same effect
could equally well be achieved by including the COMMON definition
of INDEX in A as well, even though its variables are not referenced
there.

        In general, the syntax of the SAVE statement is

        SAVE [*a*[,*a*]....]

where *a* is a local variable name, local array name, or COMMON
block name enclosed in slashes. If there is no list associated with the
SAVE statement, then all local and COMMON variables and arrays
will have their values retained. The whole problem of wondering
which entities to put into a SAVE statement can thus be resolved
quite simply by inserting a SAVE statement without a list into every
subprogram.

6. BLOCK DATA

In the examples of the DATA statement given earlier (Section 5.6),
all the quantities which were to be initialized were either local variables or arrays. In the meantime we have encountered variables and
arrays which have a larger scope, or range of validity, namely those
appearing in COMMON blocks. They too may be initialized in
DATA statements, but such statements must be collected into a special type of program unit, known as a BLOCK DATA subprogram.
It must contain nothing other than a header line, specification statements (other than INTRINSIC and EXTERNAL statements, see
below), an END statement and, of course, comment lines. An example is

```
      BLOCK DATA
      COMMON /AXES/ I,J,K
*
*   DEFINE THE INDICES OF THE COORDINATE SYSTEM
      DATA I,J,K /1,2,3/
      END
```

in which the variables in the COMMON block AXES are defined
for use in any other program unit which accesses them.

It is possible to collect many COMMON blocks and their corresponding DATA statements together in one BLOCK DATA subprogram. However, in a program consisting of well defined parts, or *modules* (see Chapter10), it may be a better practice to have several different BLOCK DATA subprograms, each containing COMMON blocks which have some logical association with one another. To allow for this eventuality, FORTRAN permits BLOCK DATA subprograms to be named in order to be able to distinguish them. A complete program may contain any number of BLOCK DATA subprograms, but only one of them may be unnamed. An example of a named BLOCK DATA subprogram header line is

BLOCK DATA START

The name may be any legal FORTRAN name.

7. Functions

Following main programs, subroutine and BLOCK DATA subprograms, we now come to the fourth type of program unit, the function subprogram. This is similar in many respects to the subroutine, but with three major differences:

i) a function returns a single value corresponding to one of the six data types and, therefore, has a different invocation;

ii) the header line declares it to be a function, and is combined with an optional type declaration for the type of value returned;

iii) the argument list of a function must not include any alternate RETURNs.

FORTRAN functions are best thought of and used as functions in the mathematical sense, providing a function value for a given set of values of the arguments. They allow programs to be well structured, in that functions which otherwise would be coded many times need to be coded only once, and can be invoked from other program units. An example is given in Ex. 11, which is a logical function, named INSIDE, which returns the value TRUE if a point given as argument is inside a circle of radius R and origin X0, Y0, and returns the value FALSE otherwise.

The example shows how, for one set of input values, a single

```
         LOGICAL INCIRC, INSIDE
         :
         INCIRC = INSIDE(3., 4., 5.)
         :
         END
         :
         LOGICAL FUNCTION INSIDE (X0, Y0, R)
    *
    *    TO DETERMINE WHETHER A POINT AT X0,Y0
    *    LIES WITHIN A CIRCLE OF RADIUS R.
         INSIDE = X0**2 + Y0**2 .LE. R**2
         END
```

Example 11

value is calculated and returned. In general, a function may contain any executable statement (apart from an alternate RETURN), and it is quite possible to write functions which change the values of their arguments, modify the values of variables in COMMON blocks, perform input/output operations *etc.* However, such coding conflicts with the good programming practice of functions having no so-called *side-effects,* that is no entity should be modified other than the result of a function itself, and any local variables. In all other cases, subroutines should be used, as they may be expected to perform complex operations whereas, when calling a function, one should be assured that nothing else goes on 'behind the scenes'.

Ex. 11 is an example of a logical function. Functions have a type in exactly the same way as a variable, *i.e.* they are real or integer depending on the first letter of their name (and any IMPLICIT statement), unless a specific type declaration is included in the header line or within the specification statements. If a function is not of the default type, then each program unit containing a reference to the function must also include the corresponding type declaration, as was shown in the example.

For functions of type CHARACTER, a length specification for the function may also be included in the header, in the same way as is done for a CHARACTER variable, for example

```
    CHARACTER*4 FUNCTION WORD(CHARS)
```

The length must not be a symbolic constant, but may be an assumed length:

CHARACTER* (*) FUNCTION TITLE(LIST)

The actual length may be obtained within the function by means of the LEN intrinsic function (see Appendix A).

7.1 Intrinsic functions

In a language which has a clear orientation towards scientific applications, there is an obvious requirement that the most frequently used mathematical functions be provided as part of the language itself, rather than expecting that every user code them individually. FORTRAN provides an extensive set of intrinsic functions, with such self-evident names as SQRT for the square-root function, MAX for the maximum of a set of values (all of a given type), SIN for the sine of an angle (in radians), *etc.* A complete list is given in Appendix A. These standard functions should be used wherever needed, in preference to writing equivalent code oneself either as in-line code in the program text or as a private function. The intrinsic functions provided by a given compiler are usually coded to be very efficient, and are typically very robust in that they are well tested over the complete range of values they are able to deal with. It is usually difficult to compete with the high standard of code provided by compiler vendors in this respect.

7.2 EXTERNAL statement

In spite of what has just been stated in the previous sub-section, there may, in fact, sometimes be occasions when it becomes necessary to override the standard FORTRAN functions. Either one may wish to try out one's own version of a function, or one wishes to make a function with one name perform a different, non-standard operation. This is a highly dangerous practice, as it is most misleading to read code which contains calls to the SIN function, only to discover later that the SIN function has been replaced by a user coded function which returns, say, the absolute value of the argument. Such freedom is allowed in FORTRAN, but should never be taken advantage of. The mechanism is the EXTERNAL statement. This may be used to declare a list of intrinsic function names, whose calls in a given program unit are not to be made to the standard set of intrinsic functions, but are to be made to externally provided functions of the same name. An extreme example is given in Ex. 12, which overrides the SQRT function with the SIN function. The EXTERNAL statement will be met again in the Section 9.

```
        :
        EXTERNAL SQRT
        :
        Y  =  SQRT(X)
        :
        END
        FUNCTION SQRT(A)
*
*       MY OWN WAY TO CODE BADLY
        SQRT  =  SIN(A)
        END
```

Example 12

8. Statement Functions

It may happen that within a single program unit there are repeated occurrences of a computation which can be represented as a single statement. For instance, to calculate the parabolic function represented by

$$y = a + bx + cx^2$$

for different values of x, but with the same coefficients, there may be references to

```
        Y1  =  1. + X1*(2. + 3.*X1)
        :
        Y2  =  1. + X2*(2. + 3.*X2)
        :
```

etc. In such cases, it is more convenient to invoke a so-called *statement function,* which is defined in one place in the program unit, and may be subsequently referenced just like a normal function. To do this, the statement function must appear after all the specification statements and before the executable statements. The example above would become

```
        PARAB(X)  =  1. + X*(2. + 3.*X)
        :
        Y1  =  PARAB(X1)
        :
        Y2  =  PARAB(X2)
```

Here, X is a dummy argument, which is used in the definition of the statement function. The variables X1 and X2 are actual arguments to the function.

Statement functions are useful for one-statement functions invoked repeatedly in a single program unit, as the body of the function appears in a single statement, which may then be more easily tested and modified. The implementation is often such that there is no overhead involved in calling the function, as the compiler substitutes the function body for the call at compile-time, creating so-called *in-line code*. This is in contrast to function subprograms, which are less efficient as they have to be called in a way which involves a transfer of control from one subprogram to another. The disadvantages of statement functions are that they are limited to one statement and to one program unit, and there are consequently relatively few applications for them.

A statement function may reference other statement functions appearing before it in the same program unit, but not any appearing after. A futher restriction is that the right-side may contain no character substring references.

9. Procedures as Arguments

In this section we shall complete the description of the arguments of subroutines and functions, by showing how the names of procedures may be passed between program units as arguments. Let us suppose, in a simple case, that a subroutine A calls another subroutine B, which in turn calls a subroutine C or D, depending on some condition. If this condition is best evaluated in A, and if C and D have identical calling sequences (or none), then the code may be written as shown in Ex. 13, where we note that C and D must be declared as external procedures.

The ability to pass procedure names is an important one when building libraries of programs which perform such tasks as generalized function fitting. It is possible to pass the name of the function in question, and to provide the function body itself, to be called by the library programs. This leads to a program structure which is like a sandwich: on the outside are two layers of code written specifically by a user, and inside is a generalized package provided by other means, perhaps as part of an installation's program library. The user's code calls the general package which in turn calls the user's own subroutines or functions. An outline example is given in Ex. 14.

```
EXTERNAL C,D
:
IF(.....) THEN
   CALL B(C)
ELSE
   CALL B(D)
ENDIF
:
END
SUBROUTINE B(SUB)
:
   CALL SUB
:
END
```

Example 13

```
EXTERNAL OWNFUN
:
CALL FITPAK(OWNFUN)
:
END
SUBROUTINE FITPAK(FUNC)
:
CALL FUNC(X)
:
END
FUNCTION OWNFUN(X)
:
OWNFUN = 1. + SIN(0.5*X)
:
END
```

Example 14

9.1 Specific names and the INTRINSIC statement

Appendix A contains a number of functions that may have arguments that are all of one type or all of another. For instance, we may write

$$A = SQRT(B)$$

and the appropriate square-root function will be invoked, depending on whether the variable B is real, double-precision or complex in type. Similarly, we may write VAL = MAX(A, B, C, D) and the correct maximum-value function will be invoked, depending on whether the variables A, B, C and D are all of type integer, real or double-precision. In these cases, the names SQRT and MAX are known as *generic names,* meaning that the appropriate function is supplied, depending on the type of the actual arguments of the function, and that a single name may be used for what are, in fact, different functions.

A complication arises if such an intrinsic function name is passed as an actual argument to another subprogram. In the called subprogram, the function will appear in the argument list with a dummy name, and the compiler cannot determine which of the possible variants should be supplied. To allow for this, each intrinsic function which has a generic name also has a corresponding set of alternative *specific names*, which must be used when passing the function names as an argument. For instance, the generic name of the intrinsic square-root function is SQRT, to which correspond the three specific names SQRT (real), DSQRT (double-precision) and CSQRT (complex). These three names may be used as alternative names to SQRT whenever the argument type justifies it, but when passed as an argument, the specific name *must* be used, and must also be declared in an INTRINSIC statement. An example is given in Ex. 15 for the double-precision square-root function DSQRT. In this example we note the contrast between the use of the generic name SQRT and the specific name DSQRT, both providing the same function.

The specific names for type conversion, lexical relationship and for choosing largest or smallest values may *not* be used as actual arguments.

Having dealt with the passing of procedure names as arguments, it is now possible to recapitulate all the possible argument types by giving the full syntax of the subroutine and function statements, which are

SUBROUTINE *name* (*arg*[,*arg*]....)]

and

[*type*] FUNCTION *name* ([*arg*[,*arg*]....])

where *name* is any valid FORTRAN name; *arg* is a variable, array or dummy procedure name, or an alternate RETURN asterisk (not

```
DOUBLE PRECISION D,E
INTRINSIC DSQRT
:
E = SQRT(D)
:
CALL SUB(DSQRT)
:
END
SUBROUTINE SUB(FUNC)
DOUBLE PRECISION X,Y
:
X = FUNC(Y)
:
END
```

Example 15

for functions); and *type* is a usual type declaration, with an optional length for type CHARACTER. In the call, a variable in the dummy argument list may correspond to a variable, an expression, an array element or character substring. A dummy procedure name may correspond to a subroutine name, an external function name or an intrinsic function name.

10. ENTRY Statement

In the examples of subprograms we have encountered so far, each one was entered at the header line, and the first statement to be executed was the first executable statement after that header line. In some cases it is useful to be able to enter a subprogram at some other point, particularly when wishing to share access to some local variables or section of code. This is possible in FORTRAN by means of the ENTRY statement. This is a statement which may appear anywhere between the header line and END line of a subprogram, to provide an alternative point of entry. The ENTRY statement may have an associated dummy argument list, exactly as the SUBROUTINE and FUNCTION statements, and these arguments may be different from those given on the SUBROUTINE or FUNCTION statement of the subprogram in which the ENTRY line appears. Except in the case of character functions, an entry may be of a different type from the type of the function itself. An ENTRY is called in exactly the same manner as a subroutine or function, depending on whether it appears in a subroutine subprogram or a function subprogram. An example is given in Ex. 16 which shows a search function with two entry points. We note that LOOKU and LOOKS are synonymous within the function, so that it is immaterial which value is set before the return.

```
        FUNCTION LOOKU(LIST, LEN, MEMBER)
*
*       TO LOCATE MEMBER IN A LIST OF LENGTH
*       LEN.
*       IF LIST IS UNSORTED, ENTRY LOOKU IS USED,
*       IF LIST IS SORTED, ENTRY LOOKS IS USED.
*
        INTEGER LIST(*)
*
        CALL SORT(LIST, LEN)
*
*       ENTRY FOR SORTED LIST
        ENTRY LOOKS(LIST, LEN, MEMBER)
*
        DO 1 LOOKU = 1, LEN
            IF (LIST(LOOKU) .GE. MEMBER) GO TO 2
      1 CONTINUE
        GO TO 3
*
*       IS MEMBER AT POSITION LOOKU
      2 IF (LIST(LOOKU). EQ. MEMBER) GO TO 9
*
*       MEMBER NOT IN LIST
      3 LOOKU = 0
*
      9 END
```

Example 16

The ENTRY statement provides a certain additional level of functionality when it is required to share local variables or section of code, but in general it can lead to untidy programming, as there are perhaps many possible routes into one subprogram, and it is not always easy to sort them out when reading the code. It is generally better to write separate subprograms which communicate through a COMMON block. In fact, code containing ENTRY statements can become quite dangerous, as is shown in the illegal code of Ex. 17. Here the entries SUB and BANG have two different argument lists, and this means that the code following an entry at BANG cannot access the array A. If, on the other hand, the subroutine is entered at SUB, and there is no return executed before ENTRY BANG, then the array A is available, but the variables K and X are not. So in either case the line indicated is illegal.

```
SUBROUTINE SUB(A)
:
DIMENSION A(*)
:
:
ENTRY BANG(K, X)
:
X = A(K)   < - illegal: either A, or K and X, are undefined
:
END
```

Example 17

11. Order of Statements

We have now met examples of all the different types of statement which the FORTRAN language contains, except for the FORMAT and some other I/O statements which will appear in the next chapter. Each time a new type of statement has been introduced, some mention has been made of the position in which it may appear in the source code, and these rules can now be summarized by their representation in Fig. 7. The order given in this figure differs slightly from that given by the standard which allows DATA statements to be freely intermingled with the executable statements, a most undesirable practice.

Many compilers interpret these rules in a lax way, but it is important to adhere to them in order to have code which is well laid out, and which is transportable to other, more strict, computer systems.

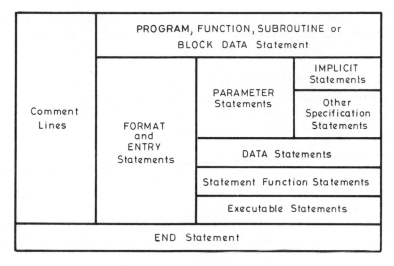

Fig. 7 Order of Statements

12. Summary

This chapter has concluded the descriptions of all FORTRAN's facilities with the exception of the input/output statements. It has introduced the four types of program unit, shown how calling sequences may be built up of various types of arguments, and how program units can also communicate through COMMON blocks. The way in which these facilities may be used to structure whole programs has been indicated. The specification and control flow statements associated with program unit communication and control have been described.

In the next chapter, which will be the last of the chapters devoted to the description of the language, we shall examine the extensive and essential facilities provided by FORTRAN for a program to communicate with storage and peripheral devices of various kinds – the input/output statements.

Exercises

1. A subroutine receives as arguments an array of values, x, and the number of elements in x, n. If the mean and variance of the values in x are given by

$$\text{mean} = (\Sigma x(i))/n$$
$$\text{variance} = (\Sigma(x(i) - \text{mean})^2)/n$$

(where i runs from 1 to n), write a subroutine which returns these calculated values as arguments. The subroutine should check for invalid values of n (zero or negative).

2. A subroutine MATMUL multiplies together two matrices A and B, whose dimensions are IxJ and JxK, respectively, returning the result in a matrix C, dimensioned IxK. Write MATMUL, given that each element of C is defined by

$$C(m,n) = \Sigma \; (A(m,l) \times B(l,n))$$

where l runs fom 1 to J. The matrices should appear as arguments to MATMUL.

3. A function RANDOM called with no argument returns a random number in the range 0.0 to 1.0, *i.e.*

$$R = RANDOM()$$

Using this function, write the subroutine SHUFFL of Ex. 9.

4. A character string consists of a sequence of letters. Write a function to rerun that letter of the string which occurs earliest in the alphabet, *e.g.* the result of applying the function to 'DGUMVETLOIC' is 'C'.

5. Write a statement function to calculate the volume of a cylinder of radius r and length l, $\pi r^2 l$, using as the value of π the result of ACOS(-1.0).

6. Choosing a simple card game of your own choice, and assuming if necessary the existence of a random number generator function, write subroutines DEAL and PLAY of Ex. 5, using COMMON blocks to communicate between them.

7 INPUT-OUTPUT

---

1. Introduction

FORTRAN 77 has, in comparison with most other high-level programming languages, a particularly rich set of facilities for input/output (I/0). The 1977 standard brought with it important new features, the need for which had already been demonstrated by their inclusion, in a non-standard way, in many FORTRAN 66 compilers. These new features include direct access files, internal files, execution-time format specification, list-directed input/output, file enquiry, and some new edit descriptors. All of these will be explained in this chapter, together with the older features.

In contrast to the foregoing chapters, the material dealt with here is very much a 'nuts and bolts' topic, about which the rules of style have little to teach us. Input/output statements often appear ungainly, and no amount of effort in layout seems to bring a neat result. A more relevant consideration is usually efficiency, which will be dealt with in more detail in Chapter 11, but whose more immediate consequences will nevertheless be remarked upon in the course of this chapter.

Input/output is an area of FORTRAN into which not all programmers need to delve very deeply. For most small-scale programs it is sufficient to know how to read a few data records containing input variables, and how to transmit to a terminal or printer the results of a calculation. In large-scale data processing, on the other hand, the programs often have to deal with huge streams of data to and from many disc and magnetic tape files, and in these cases it is essential that great attention be paid to the way in which the I/O is designed and coded, as otherwise both the execution-time and real-time spent in the program can suffer dramatically.

This chapter begins by discussing the various forms of formatted I/O, that is I/O which deals with quantities which are not handled using the internal number representation of the computer being used, but rather a coded form which can be displayed for visual inspection by the human eye. The so called *edit descriptors,* which are used to control the translation between the internal number representation and the external format, are then explained. Finally, the topics of file control, unformatted (or binary) I/O, direct access files and file enquiry are covered.

2. Formatted I/O

2.1 Number conversion

The way in which numbers are stored internally by a computer are the concern of neither the FORTRAN standard nor this book (but see, for instance, Chapter 2 of Metcalf, 1982). The standard requires only that real, integer and logical variables be stored in *numeric storage units,* and that the two parts of a double-precision or complex variable be stored in two sequential numeric storage units. A numeric storage unit normally corresponds to a computer *word,* and within this word there are normally several *fields,* each storing a particular part of the numerical information. For instance, an *integer number* is typically stored in two fields, one containing the sign of the quantity, and the other containing the magnitude. This we may picture as

S=sign bit

A *real number* is typically stored in three fields, one for the sign, one for the exponent and one for the mantissa, or fractional part. (Real numbers are not stored in the base 10 number system to which we are accustomed, but in base 2 or 16 number systems which are more convenient for a computer to manipulate). A real number is thus stored as

A *logical variable* is typically stored such that one particular value of a computer word is .TRUE. by definition, and another .FALSE. . These values may, for instance, be zero and one, respectively.

Character variables are stored, according to the standard, in a sequence of *character storage units,* one for each character in the variable. Usually, character storage units will be packed into computer words, but the number packed into one word varies from computer to computer and the standard makes no statement about how numeric storage units and character storage units relate either to one another or to the words of a computer storage system.

A computer executes the instructions specified by a program, as translated by a compiler and loader. All the operations it carries out are on operands whose values are stored in the types of internal number systems just described. If, at some stage, we wish to output one of the values − to display it on a terminal or to print it − then the internal representation must be converted into an external, or coded, representation which can be read in a normal way. For instance, the contents of a given computer word may correspond to the exact value -0.00045. For our particular purpose, we may wish to display this quantity as $-.000450$, or as $-4.5E-04$ or rounded to one significant digit as $-.5E-03$. The conversion from the internal representation to the coded external form is carried out according to the information specified by an *edit descriptor* contained in a *format specification*. These will both be dealt with fully later in this chapter; for the moment, it is sufficient to give a few examples. For instance, to print an integer value in a field of 10 characters width, we would use the edit descriptor I10, where I stands for integer conversion, and 10 specifies the width of the output field. To print a real quantity in a field of 10 characters, five of which are reserved for the fractional part of the number, we specify F10.5. F stands for floating-point (real) conversion, 10 is the total width of the output field and 5 is the width of the fractional part of the field. If the number given above were to be converted according to this edit descriptor, it would appear as -0.00045. To print a character variable in a field of 10 characters, we would specify A10, where A stands for alphanumeric conversion.

A format specification consists of one or more edit descriptors, and can be coded either as a character string, for instance

    '(I10, F10.3, A10)'

or as a separate FORMAT statement, referenced by a statement label, *e.g.*

  10 FORMAT(I10, F10.3, A10)

Note that in both cases the edit descriptors are enclosed in parentheses and separated by commas. To print the variables J, B and C, of type integer, real and character respectively, we may then write either

> PRINT '(I10, F10.3, A10)', J,B,C

or

> PRINT 10, J,B,C
> 10   FORMAT(I10, F10.3, A10)

The first form is normally used when there is only a single reference in a program unit to a given format specification, the second when there are several or when the format is complicated. The part of the statement designating the variables to be printed is known as the *output list* and forms the subject of the following section.

2.2 I/O lists

The quantities to be read or written by a program are specified in an I/O list. This consists of the names of all the quantities involved, separated by commas. (Optionally, the list may be absent.) For quantities to be read by a program, the list may consist of

  i) variable names

  ii) array names (but not those of assumed size arrays)

  iii) array elements

  iv) character substrings

  v) implied DO-lists.

For quantities to be written by a program, the list may contain all these items and, additionally, almost any valid expression. Examples, using an array A(10), an integer variable I and a character variable WORD, are

> PRINT '(I10)', I
> PRINT '(10F10.3)', A
> PRINT '(3F10.3)', A(1),A(2),A(3)
> PRINT '(A10)', WORD(5:14)

PRINT '(5F10.3)', (A(I),I = 1,9,2)
PRINT '(2F10.3)', A(1)*A(2)+I, SQRT(A(3))

where we note the use of a *repeat count* in front of those edit descriptors which are required for more than one item in the I/O list.

All these examples, except the last one, would be equally valid as input statements using the READ statement, *e.g.*

READ '(I10)', I

Such statements may be used to read values which are then assigned to the entities in the input list. How these input values are represented externally will be described in Section 7.3.

The one restriction on valid expressions is that a character expression may not include the concatenation of an operand passed as an actual argument whose length is specified by an asterisk.

2.3 Format definition

In the PRINT and READ statements of the previous sub-section, the format specification was given each time in the form of a character constant immediately following the keyword. In fact, there are four ways in which a format specification may be given. They are:

i) As a statement label, referring to a FORMAT statement containing the relevant specification:

PRINT 100, Q
:
100 FORMAT(F10.3)

The FORMAT statement must appear in the same program unit, and may be referenced any number of times. It is customary either to place each FORMAT statement immediately after the first statement which references it, or to group them all together just before the END statement. It is also customary to have a separate sequence of numbers for the statement labels used for FORMAT statements. A given FORMAT statement may be used by any number of formatted I/O statements, whether for input or for output.

ii) As a character variable, array, array element or expression:

```
          CHARACTER*(*) FORM
          PARAMETER (FORM = '(F10.3)')
          :
          PRINT FORM, Q
```

or

```
          CHARACTER CARRAY(7)
          DATA CARRAY/'(','F','1','0','.','3',')'/
          :
          PRINT CARRAY, Q
```

or

```
          CHARACTER CARRAY(10)*7
          DATA CARRAY(1)/'(F10.3)'/
          :
          PRINT CARRAY(1), Q
```

or

```
          CHARACTER CARR1(10)*4, CARR2(10)*3
          :
          CARR1(10)  =  '(F10'
          CARR2(3)  =  '.3)'
          :
          I  =  10
          J  =  3
          PRINT CARR1(I)//CARR2(J), Q
```

or simply

```
          PRINT '(F10.3)', Q
```

From these examples it may be seen that it is possible to program formats in a flexible way, and particularly that it is possible to use arrays, expressions and also substrings in a way which allows a given format to be built up dynamically at execution-time from various components. However, on input *no* component of the format specification may appear also in the input list, or be associated with it *via*, for instance, an EQUIVALENCE statement. This is because the standard requires that the whole format specification be established *before* any I/O takes place.

iii) As an integer variable to which a statement label has been assigned in an ASSIGN statement:

```
      ASSIGN 100 TO KEY
      :
      PRINT KEY, Q
  100 FORMAT(F10.3)
```

iv) As an asterisk. This is a type of I/O known as *list-directed* I/O, in which the format is defined by the computer system at the moment the statement is executed, depending on both the type and magnitude of the entities involved. This facility is particularly useful for the input and output of small quantities of values, especially in temporary code which is used for test purposes, and which is removed from the final version of the program:

$$\text{PRINT *, 'SQUARE} - \text{ROOT OF Q} = \text{', SQRT(Q)}$$

This example outputs a character constant describing the expression which is to be output, followed by the value of the expression under investigation. On the terminal screen, this might appear as

$$\text{SQUARE} - \text{ROOT OF Q} = 4.392246$$

the exact format being dependent on the computer system used. Examples for input will be given later in this section.

2.4 Unit definition

Input/output operations are used to transfer data between the variables of an executing program, as stored in computer words, and an external medium. There are many types of external media: the terminal, printer, disc drive and magnetic tape are perhaps the most familiar. Old hands at computing will remember punched cards, drums and paper tape. Whatever the device, a FORTRAN program regards each one from which it reads or to which it writes as a *unit,* and each unit, with two exceptions, has associated with it a *unit number.* This number is often in the range 1 to 99. Thus we might associate with a disc drive from which we are reading the unit number 10, and to a magnetic tape drive to which we are writing the unit number 11.

There are two I/O statements, variants of READ and PRINT, which do not reference any unit number, and these are the statements we have used so far in examples, for the sake of simplicity. A READ statement without a unit number will normally expect to read from the terminal, unless the program is working in batch (non-interactive) mode in which case there will be a disc file with a reserved name from which it reads. Old systems expected such a statement to read from a punched-card reader. A PRINT statement without a unit number will normally expect to output to the terminal, unless the program is in batch mode in which case another disc file with a reserved name will be used. Old systems would, as the name of the statement implies, print directly to paper on a line-printer. The system may implicitly associate unit numbers to these default units.

Apart from these two special cases, all I/O statements must refer explicitly to a unit number in order to identify the device to which or from which data are to be transferred. The unit number may be given in one of four forms. These are shown in the following examples which use another form of the READ containing a unit number, *u,* and format specification, *fmt,* in parentheses and separated by a comma, where *fmt* is a specifier defined as described in the previous sub-section:

READ *(u, fmt) list*

The four forms of *u* are :

i) As an explicit number:

READ (4, '(F10.3)') Q

where the number may be any integer constant allowed by the system for this purpose.

ii) As an integer expression:

READ (NUNIT, '(F10.3)') Q
READ (4*I + J, 100) A

iii) As an asterisk:

READ (*, '(F10.3)') Q
READ (*, *) A

where the asterisk implies a standard I/O unit designated by the system, usually the same as that used for READ without a unit number.

These three forms give access to certain error recovery facilities associated with I/O statements, which are not available with the simple READ and PRINT without unit number and which will be described shortly.

iv) As a character variable, array, array element or substring identifying an *internal file*. This requires more explanation, but will be familiar to those who have used the ENCODE/DECODE statements of old, non-standard FORTRAN dialects. Internal files may *not* be used for list-directed I/O.

Internal files are intended for the conversion of data from one format to another, when one of the formats involved is a character format. As such they allow format conversion between various representations to be carried out by the program in a storage area defined within the program itself. There are two particularly useful applications, one to read data whose format is not properly known in advance, and the other to prepare output lists containing mixed character and numerical data, all of which has to be prepared in character form, perhaps to be displayed as a caption on a graphics display. The first application will now be described; the second will be dealt with later in this section.

Imagine that we have to read a string of 30 digits, which might correspond to 30 one-digit integers, 15 two-digit integers or 10 three-digit integers. The information as to which type of data is involved is given by the value of a final digit, which has the value 1, 2 or 3, depending on the number of digits each integer contains. An internal file provides us with a mechanism whereby the 30 digits can be read into a character buffer area. The value of the final digit can be tested separately, and 30, 15, or 10 values read from the internal file, depending on this value. The basic code to achieve this might read as follows (no error recovery or data validation is included, for simplicity):

```
INTEGER IVAL (30)
CHARACTER BUFFER*30, FORM(3)*6
DATA FORM/'(30I1)', '(20I2)', '(10I3)'/
READ (*, '(A30,I1)') BUFFER, KEY
READ (BUFFER, FORM (KEY)) (IVAL(I), I = 1,30/KEY)
```

IVAL is an array which will receive the values, BUFFER a character

variable of a length sufficient to contain the 30 input digits, and
FORM a character array containing the three possible formats to
which the input data might correspond. The first READ statement
reads 30 digits into BUFFER as character data, and a final digit
into the integer variable KEY. The second READ statement reads
the data from BUFFER into IVAL, using the appropriate conversion
as specified by the edit descriptor selected by KEY. The number of
variables read from BUFFER to IVAL is defined by the implied
DO-loop, whose second parameter is an integer expression depending
also on KEY. After execution of this code, IVAL will contain
30/KEY values, their number and exact format not having been
known in advance.

2.5 Formatted READ

In the last two sub-sections complete descriptions of the possible
definitions of format specifications and unit numbers have been
given, using simplified forms of the READ and PRINT statements
as examples. There are, in fact, two forms of the READ statement:

READ *fmt, list*

and

READ (*u, fmt* [, IOSTAT = *ios*] [, ERR = *sl1*] [, END = *sl2*]) *list*

where *u* and *fmt* are the unit number and format specifiers
described above, and IOSTAT, ERR and END are optional keywords which allow a user to specify how a READ statement shall
recover from various exceptional conditions. These optional keywords
may be specified in any order. The unit number and format specifier, here given as *positional* keywords may also be given with
explicit keywords:

READ(UNIT = *u*,   FMT = *fmt*   [,   IOSTAT = *ios*]   [,   ERR = *sl1*]
[, END = *sl2*]) *list*

Use of keywords allows any ordering, although it is usual to keep
the unit number and format specification as the first two.

The meanings of the optional keywords, which do not apply to
internal files, are as follows. If the IOSTAT keyword is specified,
then *ios* is an integer variable or array element, which, after execution of the READ statement, has the value zero if the statement has

executed correctly, a negative value if an end-of-file condition was detected on the input device, or a positive value if any other error was detected, for instance a parity error. The actual values assigned to *ios* in the event of an exception occurring are not defined by the standard, only the signs; given computer systems may assign certain values for various conditions, as described in their compiler manuals.

If the ERR keyword is specified, then *sl1* is a statement label to which control will be transferred in the event of any exception occurring, other than end-of-file.

If the END keyword is specified, then *sl2* is a statement label to which control will be transferred in the event of an end-of-file condition being detected (see Section 7.5). The labels *sl1* and *sl2* may be the same. Most compiler systems require that these keywords be specified if execution of the program is to continue after detection of an exception. If they are not specified and an exception occurs, execution will stop. An example of a READ statement with its associated error recovery is given in Ex. 18, in which ERROR and ENDFIL are subroutines to deal with the exceptions. They will normally be system-dependent.

```
      READ (NUNIT, 10, IOSTAT = IOS, ERR = 110,
    +            END = 120)  A,B,C
*
*     Successful read  −  continue execution
      :

      :
*
*     Error condition  −  take appropriate action
  110 CALL ERROR (IOS)
      GO TO 999
*
*     END − OF − FILE condition  −  test whether more
*     files follow
  120 CALL ENDFIL
      :
   10 FORMAT(3F10.3)
  999 END
```

Example 18

It is a good practice to include some sort of error recovery in all READ statements which are included permanently in a program. Input for test purposes is normally sufficiently well handled by the simple form of READ without unit number, and without error recovery.

2.6 List-directed input

In Sub-section 7.2.3, the list-directed output facility using an asterisk as format specifier was described. This facility is equally useful for input, especially of small quantities of test data. On the input record, the various constants may appear in any of their usual forms, just as if they were being read under the usual edit descriptors, as defined in Sub-section 7.3.2 below. Two exceptions are that complex values must be enclosed in parentheses, and that the optional characters which are allowed in a logical constant (those other than T and F, see Sub-section 7.3.2) must include neither a comma nor a slash. Character constants are enclosed in apostrophes and may be spread over as many records as necessary to contain them, (records will be described further in the next section). To input an apostrophe in a character constant, it must be followed immediately by a second apostrophe.

The constants are separated in the input record by blanks or by commas. A blank embedded in a complex or character constant is not a separator. An input record may be optionally terminated by a slash (/), in which case all the following values in the record are ignored. It is possible to use a repeat count for a given constant, *e.g.* 6*10 to specify six times the integer value 10.

If there are no values between two successive separators, or between the beginning of the first record and the first separator, this is taken to represent a *null value* and the corresponding item in the input list is left unchanged, defined or undefined as the case may be. A series of null values may be represented by a repeat count without a constant: ,6*, .

Examples of this form of the READ statement are

```
LOGICAL FLAG
COMPLEX FIELD(2)
CHARACTER*4 WORD, TITLE*12
      :
READ *, I, A, FIELD, FLAG, WORD, TITLE
```

If this reads the input record

10*b*6.4*b*(1.,0.)*b*(2.,0.)*b*T*b*'TEST'

(in which *b* stands for a blank, and blanks are used as separators), then I, A, FIELD, FLAG, and WORD will acquire the values 10, 6.4, (1.,0.) and (2.,0.), .TRUE. and TEST respectively. TITLE remains unchanged. For the input records

10,.64E1,2*,.TRUE.
'VAL1'/'HISTOGRAM*b*10'

(in which commas are used as separators), the variables I, A, FLAG, and WORD will acquire the values 10, 6.4, .TRUE., and VAL1 respectively. FIELD remains unchanged, and the input string 'HISTOGRAM*b*10' is ignored as it follows a slash. Because of this slash the read statement does not continue with the next record, and the list is thus not fully satisfied. We note again that this facility cannot be used to read from an internal file.

2.7 Formatted output

There are two types of formatted output statements, the PRINT statement which has appeared in many of the examples so far in this chapter, and the WRITE statement which is similar to the full form of the READ statement. Their syntax is:

> PRINT *fmt, list*

and

> WRITE (*u, fmt* [,IOSTAT = *ios*] [,ERR = *sl1*]) *list*

where all the components have the same meanings as described for the READ statement above. A second form of the WRITE statement allows all the parameters to be specified by keywords, as is also the case for the READ statement. The end-of-file condition does not apply for WRITE statements. An example is

> WRITE (NOUT, 100, IOSTAT = IOS, ERR = 110) A
> :
> 100 FORMAT(10F10.3)

An example of a WRITE statement using an internal file is given in Ex. 19, which builds a character string from numeric and character components. The final character string might be passed to another subroutine for output, for instance as a caption on a graphics display.

In this example, a character variable is defined which is long

```
          COMMON/MONEY/IDAY, CASH
  *
          CHARACTER* 50 LINE
          :
  *
  *       WRITE INTO LINE
          WRITE (LINE,'(A, I2, A, F8.2, A)')
          +    'TAKINGS FOR DAY ', IDAY,
          +    ' ARE ', CASH, ' DOLLARS'
```

Example 19

enough to contain the text to be transferred to it. The WRITE
statement contains a format specification with A edit descriptors
without a field width. These assume a field width corresponding to
the actual length of the character strings to be converted. After execution of the WRITE statement, LINE might contain the character
string

   TAKINGS FOR DAY 3 ARE   4329.15 DOLLARS

and this could be used as a string for further processing.

2.8 Carriage control

The FORTRAN formatted output statements were originally designed
for line-printers, with their concept of lines and pages of output. In
order to be able to control the mechanical motion of the printer
carriage, the first character of each output record is not printed but
interpreted as a *carriage control character*. If it is a blank, no action
is taken, and it is good practice to insert a blank as the first character of each record, either explicitly as ' ' or using the T2 edit
descriptor (described in the next section), in order to avoid inadvertent generation of spurious character control characters. This can
happen when the first character in an output record is non-blank,
and might occur, for instance, when printing integer values with the
format

   100 FORMAT(I5)

Here all output values between -999 and 9999 will have a blank in
the first position, but all others will generate a character there which
may be used for carriage control.

The carriage control characters defined by the standard are:

+   to remain on the same line (overprint)
0   to double space
1   to advance to the beginning of the next page

It should be noted, however, that many compilers allow a larger set of carriage control characters than this.

3. Edit Descriptors

In the description of the possible forms of a format specification in Section 7.2, a few examples of the edit descriptors were given. As mentioned there, an edit descriptor is a precise specification of how a numerical or other type of value is to be converted into a character string on an output device or internal file, or converted from a character string on an input device or internal file to an internal representation. Another concept which we shall meet again in this section is that of a *record* or sequence of values forming a unit of data transfer. Each time an output statement is executed, the quantities transmitted become the elements of one or more records. A record may be empty (if there is no output list). A collection of records is known as a *file*.

There are two types of file organization, *sequential* and *direct access*. A sequential file may be considered as an ordered sequence of records which has a beginning and an end. The end of the file is indicated by an *end-of-file* marker. When reading a sequential file, a single READ statement will cause the contents of one or more records to be transferred to the input list. The file will then be positioned in front of the following record. If there is no further record, the file will instead be positioned in front of the end-of-file marker, so that an attempt to read another record will cause the end-of-file condition to arise, as described previously. Direct access file will be described in Section 7.6.

3.1 Repeat counts

Edit descriptors fall into two classes: the *repetitive* and the *non-repetitive*. The repetitive edit descriptors may be preceded by a repeat count (an unsigned integer constant), such as we have already met in examples, *e.g.*

10F12.3

The non-repetitive edit descriptors do not have an associated repeat count. A repeat count may be applied to a group of edit descriptors, enclosed in parentheses:

PRINT '(4(I5,F8.2))', (I(J), A(J), J = 1,4)

This is equivalent to writing

PRINT '(I5,F8.2,I5,F8.2,I5,F8.2,I5,F8.2)', (I(J), A(J), J = 1,4)

Repeat counts such as this may be nested:

PRINT '(2(2I5,2F8.2))', I(1),I(2),A(1),A(2),I(3),I(4),A(3),A(4)

If an I/O list contains more elements than the number of edit descriptors in the format specification, taking account of repeat counts, then a new record will begin, and the format specification repeated, and so on until the list is exhausted. To print an array of 100 integer elements, 10 elements to a line, the following statement might be used:

PRINT '(10I8)', (I(J), J = 1,100)

Similarly, when reading from an input file, new records would be read until the full list is satisfied, a new record being taken from the input file each time the specification is repeated *even if the individual records contain more input data than specified by the format specification*. This superfluous data would be ignored. For example, reading the two records (*b* again stands for a blank)

bbb10bbb15bbb20
bbb25bbb30bbb35

under control of the READ statement

READ '(2I5)', I,J,K,L

would result in the four variables I, J, K and L acquiring the values 10, 15, 25 and 30, respectively.

If a FORMAT statement contains several components in parentheses, as in

100 FORMAT(2I5, 3(I2,2(I1,I3)), (2F8.2,I2))

then the whole format statement will be used once, and then the right-most part in first-level parentheses, here (2F8.2,I2), will be repeated as often as necessary until the list is exhausted. Each repeat of the specification in these first-level parentheses will cause a new record to be read.

3.2 Repetitive edit descriptors

Integer values may be converted by means of the I edit descriptor. This comes in a basic form, Iw, which defines the width of a field, w, a non-zero unsigned integer constant. The integer value will be read from or written to this field, adjusted to its right-hand side. If we again designate a blank position by b then the value -99 printed under control of the edit descriptor I5 will appear as $bb-99$, the sign counting as one position in the field.

An alternative form of this edit descriptor for output allows the number of digits which are to be printed to be specified exactly, even if some are leading zeros. The form I$w.m$ specifies the width of the field, w, and the number of digits to be output, m, an unsigned integer constant. The value 99 printed under control of the edit descriptor I5.3 would appear as bb099.

For the I and all other numeric edit descriptors, if the output field is too narrow to contain the number to be output, it is filled with asterisks.

Real values may be converted by either E or F edit descriptors. The F descriptor we have met in earlier examples. Its general form is F$w.d$, where d an unsigned integer constant which defines the number of digits to appear after the decimal point in the output field. The decimal point counts as one position in the field. On input, the number of digits actually appearing after the decimal point will override any value of d which might be specified. Reading the value $b9.3729b$ with the edit descriptor F8.3 would cause the value 9.3729 to be transferred. These digits may appear anywhere in the input field, as the decimal point overrides the d part of the descriptor, and all the following digits are transferred. Trailing digits will be lost only if the input value is rounded because it contains, in total, more digits than the number of significant digits which can be stored in a word on the computer being used.

There are, in addition, two other forms of input string which are acceptable to the F edit descriptor. The first is a signed string of digits without a decimal point. In this case, the d right-most digits will be taken to be the fractional part of the value. Thus

$b-14629$ read under control of the edit descriptor F7.2 will transfer the value -146.29. The second form is the standard real or double-precision form of constant, as defined in Section 2.6. In this case, the decimal point again overrides the d part of the descriptor. Thus the value 14.629E$-$2 under control of the edit descriptor F9.1 will transfer the value 0.14629.

Values are rounded on output following the normal rules of arithmetic. Thus, the value 10.9336, when output under control of the edit descriptor F8.3, will appear as bb10.934, and under the control of F4.0 as b11. .

The alternative E edit descriptor has two forms, and is more appropriate for numbers with a magnitude below about 0.01, or above 1000. The rules for these two forms for input are identical to those for the F edit descriptor — the two edit descriptors E and F are interchangeable. For output a different character string will be transferred, containing an exponent field of four characters, consisting for the E$w.d$ form of the descriptor of either E followed by a sign and two digits, or of a sign and three digits, depending on the size of the exponent. Thus, for $1.234*10^{23}$ converted by the edit descriptor E10.4, the string b.1234E$+$24 will be transferred. The same edit descriptor would cause the value $1.234*10^{-150}$ to be transferred as b.1234$-$149, (some compilers print an optional zero before the decimal point).

The second form of the E edit descriptor is E$w.d$Ee, where e is an unsigned, non-zero integer constant, which determines the number of digits to appear in the exponent field. This form is obligatory for exponents whose magnitude is greater than 999. Thus the value $1.234*10^{1234}$ would require an edit descriptor like E12.4E4 to transfer the string b.1234E$+$1235. An increasing number of computers are able to deal with these very large exponent ranges.

Double-precision values are formatted under control of the D$w.d$ edit descriptor. On input, the forms are exactly as described for the F edit descriptor. On output, the form is either identical to that described for E editing, or has a D in place of the E in the exponent field, depending on the processor.

General real values can be formatted also with the G$w.d$ and G$w.d$Ee edit descriptors. These are identical to the E edit descriptor forms on input, and similar on output with the exception that if the size of the d field allows and if the value is greater than 0.1 in magnitude, the value will be converted as though under control of an appropriate F edit descriptor. This form is useful for printing values whose magnitudes are not well known in advance, and where an F conversion is preferred where possible, and an E otherwise.

Complex values may be edited under control of pairs of F, E, G or D edit descriptors. The two parts of the pair do not need to be identical. The complex value (0.1,100.) converted under control of F6.1,E8.1 would appear as *bbb*0.1*b*0.1E+03 . The two parts of the pair may be separated by one or more of the non-repetitive edit descriptors to be described below.

Logical values may be edited using the L*w* edit descriptor. This defines a field of width *w* which on input must contain the character T or F. This character may be preceded by blanks and a decimal point, and may be followed by any other characters. Thus a field defined by L7 permits the strings .TRUE. and .FALSE. to be input. The characters T or F will be transferred as the values .TRUE. or .FALSE. respectively. On output, the character T or F will appear in the right-most position in the output field.

Character values may be edited using the A edit descriptor in one of its two forms, either A or A*w*. In the first of the two forms, the width of the input or output field is determined by the actual width of the item in the I/O list. Thus, a character variable of length 10, containing the value STATEMENTS, when written under control of the A edit descriptor would appear in a field 10 characters wide. If, however, it were converted under an A11 edit descriptor, the variable would be printed with a leading blank, *b*STATEMENTS. Under control of A8, the eight left-most characters only would be written, STATEMEN.

Conversely, with the same variable on input, an A11 edit descriptor would cause the 10 right-most characters in the 11 character-wide input field to be transferred, *b*STATEMENTS would become STATEMENTS. The A8 edit descriptor would cause the eight characters in the field to be transferred to the eight left-most positions in the variable, and the remaining two would be filled with blanks, STATEMENT would become STATEMEN*bb*.

3.3 Non-repetitive edit descriptors

It is sometimes necessary to give other instructions to an I/O device than just the width of fields and how the contents of these fields are to be interpreted. For instance, it may be that one wishes to position fields at certain columns on the terminal screen, or to start a new record without issuing a new WRITE command. For this type of purpose, the non-repetitive edit descriptors provide a means of informing the processor which action has to be taken. Some of these edit descriptors contain information which is used as it is processed, others are like switches, which change the conditions under which I/O takes place from the point where they are encountered, until the end of the processing of the I/O statement containing them (including implicit repeats). These latter descriptors we shall deal with first.

Embedded blanks in numeric input fields are treated in one of two ways, either as zero, or as null characters which are squeezed out by moving the other characters in the input field to the right, and adding leading blanks to the field (unless the field is totally blank, in which case it is interpreted as zero). Whether blanks are treated as null characters or as zeros depends on two conditions:

i) whether or not the file concerned has been opened using an OPEN statement (see Section 7.7 below);

ii) whichever default is defined by the compiler, if no OPEN statement has been executed.

If an OPEN statement has been executed for the file, the default for that file will be as defined by that statement; if no OPEN statement has been executed the default is defined by a given compiler. Whatever the default may then be for a file, it may be overridden during a given format conversion by the BN and BZ edit descriptors. Let us suppose that the default is that blanks are treated as zeros. The input string $bb1b4$ converted by the edit descriptor I5 would transfer the value 104. The same string converted by BN,I5 would give 14. The BN switches the default for the rest of that format specification, or until a BZ edit descriptor is met, which switches it back again. The converse is true if the supposed default is that blanks are treated as null characters.

Leading signs on output are written always for negative numerical values. For positive quantities, whether the signs are written depends on a compiler default condition. Let us suppose that the default is to suppress leading plus signs, *i.e.* the value 99 printed by I5 is $bbb99$. To switch on plus sign printing the SP (sign print) edit descriptors may be used: the same number written by SP,I5 becomes $bb+99$. This option will remain in force for the remainder of the format specification, unless the SS (sign suppress) edit descriptor is met. The converse is true if the supposed default is that leading plus signs are printed. Whatever mode a format specification is in, it may be returned to the compiler default mode by means of the edit descriptor S. These edit descriptors provide complete control over sign printing, and are useful for producing coded outputs which have to be compared automatically, on two different computers.

Scale factors are the last of the switch type edit descriptors. They apply to the I/O of real quantities under the E, F, D and G edit descriptors, and are a means of scaling input, or F output. Their form is kP, where k is the scale factor. The default value of k is zero. The effect on input is that any quantity which does not have an exponent field will be reduced by a factor 10^k. On output, under control of an F edit descriptor, the quantity will be multiplied by a factor 10^k. Thus, the number 10.39 output by an 2PF6.0 edit descriptor will appear as b1039. .

On output with E and D edit descriptors, and with G where the E style editing is taken, the quantity is transferred with the exponent reduced by k, and the real part multiplied by 10^k. Thus $0.31*10^3$ written under control of 2PE9.2 will appear as $31.00E+01$. This gives a better control over the output style of real quantities which otherwise would have no significant digits before the decimal point.

Character strings can be transferred to an output file by one of three methods:

i) writing a character string under the A edit descriptor (or an asterisk), or embedding it in the format specification itself:

PRINT '(A)', ' THIS IS A STRING'

or

PRINT '('' THIS IS A STRING'')'

ii) embedding the string in a FORMAT statement, enclosed as usual in apostrophes:

100 FORMAT(' THIS IS A FORMAT STATEMENT')

this string will appear each time a PRINT 100 statement is executed;

iii) embedding the string as in the last example, but using the now obsolescent method of the so-called Hollerith string, which is mentioned here for the sake of completeness only: the output string is preceded by an nH edit descriptor, where n is the number of characters in the following string (blanks being significant):

100 FORMAT(23HI MUST COUNT CHARACTERS)

The first method should be used when a given string is printed at one place only in a program unit and the second where the string is printed from several places. The third method should never be used, being just another of FORTRAN's relics.

Tabulation in an input or output field can be achieved using the three edit descriptors Tn, TRn and TLn. These state respectively, that the next part of the I/O of the current record should begin at position n in the record, or at n positions to the right of the current position, or at n positions to the left of the current position. Let us suppose that we read an input record bb9876 with the following statement:

READ (*, '(T3, I4, TL4, I1, I2)') I, J, K

The format specification will move a notional pointer firstly to position 3, whence I will be read. I will acquire the value 9876, and the notional pointer is then at position 7. The edit descriptor TL4 moves it left four positions, back to position 3. The quantities J and K are then read, and they acquire the values 9 and 87, respectively. These edit descriptors allow replacement on output, or multiple reading of the same items in a record on input.

Spaces may be skipped in an input record or written in an output record by means of the nX edit descriptor. This moves a notional pointer in the record by n places to the right, and is equivalent to the TRn edit descriptor. To start an output record with a blank by this method, one writes

100 FORMAT(1X,....)

Spaces such as this can often be embedded as part of a repetitive edit descriptor, but 1X,I5 is not, for instance, exactly equivalent to I6 on output, as any value requiring the full six positions in the field will not have them available in the former case.

The X edit descriptor (and the T descriptors) never cause replacement of a character already in an output record, but merely cause a change in the position within the record such that such a replacement might be caused by a subsequent edit descriptor.

New records may be started at any point in a format specification by means of the slash (/) edit descriptor. This edit descriptor has no repeat counts; to skip, say, three records one must write ///. On input, a new record will be started each time a / is encountered, even if the contents of the current record have not all been transferred. Reading the two records

    bbb99bbb10
    bb100bbb11

with the statement

    READ '(BZ,I5,I3/I5,I3,I2)',I,J,K,L,M

will cause the values 99, 0, 100, 0 and 11 to be transferred to the five variables, respectively. This edit descriptor does not need to be separated by a comma from other edit descriptors.

The result of writing with a format containing a sequence of, say, three slashes, such as

    PRINT '(I5///I5)',I,J

is to separate the two values by two empty records (the last slash starts the record containing J); if I and J have the values 99 and 100, they would appear as

    bbb99
    b
    b
    bb100

A slash edit descriptor written to an internal file will cause the following values to be written to the next element of the character array specified for the file.

Colon editing is a means of terminating format control if there are no further items in an I/O list. In particular, it is useful for preventing further output of character strings used for annotation if the output list is exhausted. Consider the following output statement, for an array LEG(3):

```
   PRINT '(''LEG1 = '',I5: ''LEG2 = '',I5: ''LEG3 = '',I5)'
+    ,(LEG(I), I=1,N)
```

If N has the value 3, then three values are printed. If N has the value 1 then, without the colons, the following output string would be printed:

LEG1 = 59 LEG2 =

The colon, however, stops the processing of the format, so that the annotation for the absent second value is not printed.

4. Unformatted I/O

The whole of this chapter has so far dealt with the details of formatted I/O, in which the internal representation of a value differs from the external form, which is a character string contained in an input or output record. As we have seen, the use of formatted I/O involves an overhead for the conversion between the two forms, and usually a loss of significance too. There is also the disadvantage that the external representation occupies more space on a storage medium than the internal representation. These three actual or potential drawbacks are all absent when unformatted I/O is used. In this form, the internal representation of a value is written exactly as it stands to the storage medium, and can be read back directly with neither loss of significance nor conversion overhead. This type of I/O should be used in all cases where the input records are generated by a program on one computer, to be read back on a computer of the same type. Since internal number representations vary from one type of computer to another it is not, in general, possible to write unformatted records on one computer for reading directly on another. Only in this particular case, or when the data have to be visualized in one form or another, should formatted I/O be used.

Unformatted I/O has the incidental advantage of being simpler to program. No complicated format statements are required, and the forms of the READ and WRITE statements are the same as for formatted I/O, but with the *fmt* or FMT=*fmt* parameter omitted, as in

READ (*u* [,IOSTAT=*ios*] [,ERR=*sl1*] [,END=*sl2*]) *list*

and

WRITE (u [,IOSTAT $= ios$] [,ERR $= sl1$]) *list*

for their positional unit number forms.

5. File Control Statements

When reading or writing sequential files, whether formatted or unformatted, it is sometimes necessary to perform other control functions on the file in addition ·to input and output. In particular, one may wish to re-position the file in front of the record which has just been written or read, or back go to the start of the file, or mark the current position of the file so that it may be found again. The following three statements are provided for these purposes.

The BACKSPACE statement

It can happen in a program that a series of records is being written and that, for some reason, the last record written should be replaced by a new one, *i.e.* it should be overwritten. Similarly, when reading records, it may be necessary to re-read the last record read, or to check read a record which has just been written. For this purpose, FORTRAN provides the BACKSPACE statement, which has the syntax BACKSPACE u, or

BACKSPACE (u [,IOSTAT $= ios$] [,ERR $= sl$])

where u is the unit number as defined earlier in Section 7.2.4 (but *not* an asterisk), and the other optional parameters have the same meaning as for a READ statement. The action of this statement is to position the file in front of the last record written or read. An attempt to backspace when already positioned at the beginning of a file results in no change in the file's position. A series of BACKSPACE statements will backspace over the corresponding number of records. This statement is often very costly in computer resources and should be used as little as possible. We note that it is not possible to backspace over a record written by a list-directed output statement (Section 7.2.3).

The REWIND statement

In an analogous fashion to re-reading or re-writing or check-reading a record, a similar operation may be carried out on a complete file. For this purpose the REWIND statement, REWIND u, or

REWIND (*u* [,IOSTAT = *ios*] [,ERR = *sl*])

may be used to re-position a file, specified by the unit number *u*, at its beginning. If the file is already at its beginning, there is no change in the file's position.

The ENDFILE statement

The end of a file is normally marked by a special record which is identified as such by the computer hardware, and most computer systems ensure that all files written by a program are correctly terminated by such an end-of-file marker. In doubtful situations or when a subsequent program step will re-read the file, it is possible to write an end-of-file marker explicitly using the ENDFILE statement: ENDFILE *u*, or

ENDFILE (*u* [,IOSTAT = *ios*] [,ERR = *sl*])

where *u*, once again, is the unit number. This end-of-file marker, if subsequently read by a program, must be handled using the END = *sl* parameter of the READ statement, otherwise program execution will normally terminate. It is possible to backspace across an end-of-file marker.

Many computer systems recognize two consecutive end-of-file markers as indicating end of information on the unit in question, and any data written after a double end-of-file can never be read (although this is not specified by the standard). By contrast, single end-of-file markers provide a convenient means of grouping records into a larger logical grouping, except in the case of direct access files (see next section) from which no records can be re-read if they are written once an ENDFILE statement on the file has been executed.

We note that if a file is connected to a unit, but does not exist for the program, it will be made to exist by executing an ENDFILE statement on the unit (see Section 7.7).

6. Direct Access Files

The only type of file organization that we have so far dealt with is the sequential file, which has a beginning and an end, and which contains a sequence of records, one after the other. FORTRAN permits another type of file organization known as *direct access* (or sometimes as random access or indexed). Such files have no notion of beginning or end, nor of order or position of records. Instead, each record is identified solely by an index number, and it is possible to write, read or re-write any specified record without regard to position. (In a sequential file, only the last record or records may be rewritten; in general, records in sequential files cannot be replaced).

By default, any file used by a FORTRAN program is a sequential file, unless declared to be direct access. This declaration has to be made using the ACCESS = 'DIRECT' and RECL = rl parameters of the OPEN statement, which is described in the next section, (rl is the maximum length of a record in the file). Once this declaration has been made, reading and writing, whether formatted or unformatted, proceeds as described for sequential files, except for the addition of a REC = i parameter to the READ and WRITE statements, where i is the index number of the record concerned. A sequence of statements to write, read and replace a given record is given in Ex. 20.

```
        PARAMETER (NUNIT = 2, LEN = 100)
        :
        REAL A(LEN), B(LEN + 1:2*LEN)
        :
        OPEN (NUNIT, ACCESS = 'DIRECT', RECL = LEN)
        :
*
*       WRITE ARRAY B TO DIRECT ACCESS FILE IN
*       RECORD 14
        WRITE (NUNIT, REC = 14) B
        :
*
*       READ THE ARRAY BACK INTO ARRAY A
        READ (NUNIT, REC = 14) A
        :
        DO 1 I = 1, LEN/2
           A(I) = I
      1 CONTINUE
*
*       REPLACE MODIFIED RECORD
        WRITE (NUNIT, REC = 14) A
```

Example 20

Direct access files are particularly useful for applications which involve lots of hopping around inside a file, or where records need to be replaced, for instance in data base applications. A weakness is that the maximum length of the records must be known and specified in advance, (but a portable package to circumvent this problem is available (Matthews, 1983)).

This simple and powerful facility allows much clearer control logic to be written than is the case for a sequential file which is repeatedly read, backspaced or rewound. Only when direct access files become large may problems of long access times become evident on many computer systems, and this point should always be investigated before heavy investments are made in programming large direct access file applications.

7. I/O Status Statements

So far in this chapter we have discussed the topic of files in a rather superficial way. In the examples of the various I/O statements, an implicit assumption has always been made that the specified file was actually available, and that records could be written to it and read from it, and that, for sequential files, it could be positioned. In fact, these assumptions are not necessarily valid. In order to define explicitly and to test the status of files, three file status statements are provided: OPEN, CLOSE and INQUIRE. With the description of these three statements, the full potential of FORTRAN I/O will have been covered, but before beginning, two new definitions are required.

As we have seen in Chapter 1, a computer system contains, among other components, a CPU and a storage system. Modern storage systems are usually based on some form of disc, which is used to store files for long or short periods of time. The execution of a computer program is, by comparison, a transient event. A file may exist for years, whereas programs run for only seconds or minutes. In FORTRAN terminology, a file is said to *exist* not in the sense we have just used, but in the restricted sense that it exists as a file *to which the program might have access.* In other words, the program must not be prohibited from using the file because of a password protection system, or because some necessary action has not been taken in the job control language which is controlling the execution of the program.

A file which exists for a running program may or may not be *connected* to that program. The file is connected if it is associated with a unit number known to the program. Such connection is usually made by executing an OPEN statement for the file, but many computer systems will *pre-connect* certain files which any program may be expected to use, such as terminal input and output. Thus we see that a file may exist but not be connected. It may also be connected but not exist. This can happen for a pre-connected new file. The file will only come into existence if some other action is taken on the file: an OPEN, WRITE, PRINT or ENDFILE.

This whole area is somewhat system-dependent, and the reader is referred to the relevant compiler manuals to discover exactly what happens on the computer he or she is actually using. The general forms of the status statements follow.

7.1 OPEN statement

The OPEN statement is used to connect an external file to a unit number, the same unit number as will be used in the subsequent I/O operations on the file. The statement should be used to connect all files which have not been pre-connected by the system in use. On some systems, the execution of an OPEN statement in a program may require some corresponding action in the job control language. The syntax is

OPEN (u, *olist*)

where u is one of the forms (other than an asterisk) allowed for an external file unit number (see Section 7.2.4), and *olist* is a list of optional parameters. They are

IOSTAT = *ios*

where *ios* is an integer variable which is set to zero if the statement is correctly executed, and to a positive value otherwise.

ERR = *sl*

where *sl* is the label of a statement in the same program unit to which control will be transferred in the event of an error occurring during execution of the statement.

FILE = *fln*

where *fln* is a character expression which, ignoring any trailing blanks, is the external name of the file, which must be a valid name on the computer being used. If this parameter is omitted, the file name connected to the unit will depend on the computer system.

STATUS = *st*

where *st* is a character expression which, ignoring any trailing blanks, has the value OLD, NEW, SCRATCH or UNKNOWN. If OLD is specified, the file must already exist; if NEW is specified, the file must not already exist, but will be brought into existence by the action of the OPEN statement. The status of the file then becomes OLD. In either case, the FILE parameter must be specified.

If the value SCRATCH is specified, the file becomes connected, but it cannot be kept after completion of the program by execution of a CLOSE statement (whose description follows). The FILE parameter (above) must not be present.

If UNKNOWN is specified, the status of the file is system-dependent. This is the default of the parameter, if it is omitted.

ACCESS = *acc*

where *acc* is a character expression which, ignoring trailing blanks, has the value SEQUENTIAL or DIRECT. This value must be an allowed value for a file which already exists. If the file does not already exist, it will be brought into existence with the appropriate access method. If this parameter is omitted, the value SEQUENTIAL will be assumed.

FORM = *fm*

where *fm* is a character expression which, ignoring trailing blanks, has the value FORMATTED or UNFORMATTED. This value must be an allowed value for a file which already exists. If the file does not already exist, it will be brought into existence with the appropriate form. If this parameter is omitted, the file will be assumed to be formatted if it is a sequential file, or unformatted if it is a direct access file.

RECL = *rl*

where *rl* is an integer expression whose value must be positive. It specifies the maximum length of records for direct access files, and is obligatory for them. The parameter must be omitted if the file is sequential. For formatted files, *rl* is given in characters, and for unformatted files it is system-dependent but is usually in words. In either case, for a file which already exists the value specified must be allowed for that file. If the file does not already exist the file will be brought into existence with that value.

BLANK = *bl*

where *bl* is a character expression which, ignoring trailing blanks, has the value NULL or ZERO. This parameter sets the default for the interpretation of blanks in numeric input fields, as discussed in the description of the BN and BZ edit descriptor (Section 7.3). If the value is NULL, such blanks will be ignored (except that a completely blank field is interpreted as zero). If the value is ZERO embedded blanks will be interpreted as zeros. The effect of this parameter can always be overridden in a given format specification by the BN or BZ edit descriptor, as appropriate. If the parameter is omitted, the default is set to NULL. If the file is pre-connected and no OPEN statement is executed for that file, the default is system-dependent.

An example of an OPEN statement is

```
    OPEN (2, IOSTAT = IOS, ERR = 99, FILE = 'CITIES',
  +    STATUS = 'NEW', ACCESS = 'DIRECT', RECL = 100)
```

which brings into existence a new, direct access, unformatted file named CITIES, whose records may be up to 100 words long. The file is connected to unit number 2. Failure to execute the statement correctly will cause control to be passed to the statement labelled 99, where the value of IOS may be tested.

The OPEN statements in a program are best collected together in one place, so that any changes which might have to be made to them when transporting the program from one system to another can be carried out without having to search for them.

The purpose of the OPEN statement is to connect a file to a unit. If the unit is, however, already connected to a file then the action may be different. If the file in question does not exist, but is pre-connected, then all the parameters of the OPEN statement may be used, as above. If, however, the file exists already, then of the existing file attributes only the BLANK parameter may be modified. If a file is already connected to a unit, and another, unconnected existing or non-existing file is then connected to the same unit, the effect of the OPEN statement includes the action of a prior CLOSE statement on that unit (without a STATUS parameter, see below). A file already connected to one unit cannot also be connected to another unit. In general, by repeated execution of the OPEN statement on the same unit, it is possible to process in sequence an arbitrarily high number of files, whether they exist or not, as long as the restrictions just noted are observed.

7.2 CLOSE statement

The purpose of the CLOSE statement is to disconnect a file from a unit. Its form is

CLOSE (u [,IOSTAT = ios] [,ERR = sl] [,STATUS = st])

where u, ios and sl have the same meanings as described above for the OPEN statement.

The function of the STATUS parameter is to determine what will happen to the file once it is disconnected. The value of st, which is a character expression, may be either KEEP or DELETE, ignoring any trailing blanks. If the value is KEEP, a file which exists continues to exist after execution of the CLOSE statement, and may then, for instance, be connected again to a unit. If the value is DELETE, the file no longer exists after execution of the statement. In either case, the unit is free to be connected again to a file. The CLOSE statement may appear anywhere in the program, and if executed for a non-existing or unconnected unit, acts as a 'do nothing' statement. The value KEEP must not be specified for files with the status SCRATCH.

If the STATUS parameter is omitted, its value is assumed to be KEEP for all files, except for those whose status is SCRATCH for which the value DELETE is assumed.

An example of a CLOSE statement is

CLOSE (2, IOSTAT = IOS, ERR = 99, STATUS = 'DELETE')

7.3 INQUIRE statement

The status of a file can be defined by the operating system prior to execution of the program, or by the program itself during execution, either by an OPEN statement or by some action on a pre-connected file which brings it into existence. At any time during the execution of a program it is possible to inquire about the status and attributes of a file using the INQUIRE statement. Using a variant of this statement, it is similarly possible to determine the status of a unit, for instance whether the unit number exists for that system (*i.e.* is an allowed unit number), or whether the unit number has a file connected to it, and which attributes that file has.

Some of the attributes which may be determined by use of the INQUIRE statement are dependent on others. For instance, if a file is not connected to a unit, it is not meaningful to inquire about the access method allowed for that file. If this is nevertheless attempted, the relevant parameter is undefined.

The two variants are known as INQUIRE by file and INQUIRE by unit. With the former, the status and attributes of a named file can be determined, including if appropriate the number of the unit to which it is connected, if it is connected. With the latter variant, the status of a unit and the attributes of any file connected to it may be determined. In the description of the INQUIRE statement which follows, the two variants will be described together. Their forms are

INQUIRE ($u, ilist$)

for INQUIRE by unit, where u is an external unit specifier, and

INQUIRE (FILE $= fln$, $ilist$)

for INQUIRE by file, where fln is a character expression whose value, ignoring any trailing blanks, is the name of the file concerned. The parameter list, *ilist*, is in five sections, reflecting the dependence of certain parameters upon others. The first four parameters may always be specified but, like all the others, they are optional.

i) The *general parameters* are

IOSTAT $=$ *ios* and ERR $=$ *sl*

which both have the meaning described for the OPEN statement above, and

EXIST = *ex* and OPENED = *op*

where *ex* and *op* are both logical variables or array elements. The value of *ex* is true if the file (or unit) exists, and false otherwise. The value of *op* is true if the file (or unit) is connected to a unit (or file), and false otherwise.

ii) The following parameters give valid results *only if the file (or unit) exists:*

NAMED = *nmd* and NAME = *nam*

where *nmd* is a logical variable or array element, which has the value true if the file has a name, and false otherwise. If *nmd* is true, then the character variable or array element *nam* will contain the name of the file. This value is not necessarily the same as that given in the FILE parameter, if used, but may be qualified in some way. However, in all cases it is a name which is valid for use in a subsequent OPEN statement, and so the INQUIRE can be used to determine the actual name of a file before connecting it.

SEQUENTIAL = *seq* and DIRECT = *dir*

where *seq* and *dir* are character variables or array elements, which are assigned the value YES, NO or UNKNOWN, depending on whether the file *may* be opened for sequential or direct access respectively, or whether this cannot be determined.

FORMATTED = *fmt* and UNFORMATTED = *unf*

where *fmt* and *unf* are character variables or array elements which are assigned the value YES, NO or UNKNOWN, depending on whether the file *may* be opened for formatted or unformatted access, respectively, or whether this cannot be determined.

iii) The following parameters give valid results *only if the file (or unit) is connected:*

FORM = *frm*

where *frm* is a character variable or array element which is assigned the value FORMATTED or UNFORMATTED, depending on the form for which it is actually connected.

NUMBER = *num*

where *num* is an integer variable or array element which is assigned the value of the unit number connected to the file.

ACCESS = *acc*

where *acc* is a character variable or array element which is assigned the value SEQUENTIAL or DIRECT, depending on the access method for which the file is actually connected.

iv) The following parameters give valid results *only if the access is direct:*

RECL = *rec*

where *rec* is an integer variable or array element which is assigned the value of the maximum record length allowed for the file. The units of length are characters for formatted files, and system-dependent, but usually words, for unformatted files.

NEXTREC = *nr*

where *nr* is an integer variable or array element, which is assigned the value of the number of the last record read, plus one. If no record has been yet read, *nr* is assigned the value 1.

v) The final parameter gives a valid result *only if the file is formatted:*

BLANK = *bl*

where *bl* is a character variable or array element which is assigned the value NULL or ZERO, depending on whether the blanks in numeric fields are to be interpreted as null fields or zeros, respectively.

An example of the INQUIRE statement, for the file opened as an example of the OPEN statement above, is

```
LOGICAL EX, OP
CHARACTER *11 NAM, ACC, SEQ, FRM
INQUIRE (2, ERR = 99, EXIST = EX, OPENED = OP,
+   NAME = NAM, ACCESS = ACC, SEQUENTIAL = SEQ,
+   FORM = FRM, RECL = IREC, NEXTREC = NR)
```

After successful execution of this statement, the variables provided will have been assigned the following values:

EX	.TRUE.
OP	.TRUE.
NAM	CITIES*bbbbb*
ACC	DIRECT*bbbbb*
SEQ	NO*bbbbbbbbb*
FRM	UNFORMATTED
IREC	100
NR	1 (assuming no intervening read or write operations)

The three I/O status statements just described are perhaps the most indigestible of all FORTRAN statements, and form part of the area of the language which is the most involved. They provide, however, a powerful and portable facility for the dynamic allocation and de-allocation of files, completely under program control, which is far in advance of those found in any other programming language suitable for scientific applications.

8. Summary

This chapter has described the whole of FORTRAN's extensive I/O facilities. It has covered the formatted I/O statements, and their associated format specifications, and then turned to unformatted I/O file control statements, direct access files and finally the status statements. In order to keep this exposition to a reasonable length, no attempt has been made to provide more than a brief example of each feature.

In this difficult area, more than any other, it is important to gain experience by writing code to perform different I/O functions, and the contents of this chapter provide a complete reference to all the facilities available.

Exercises

1. Write suitable PRINT statements to print the name and contents of each of the following arrays:

    a) REAL GRID(10,10), 10 elements to a line (assuming the values are between 1.0 and 100.0);
    b) INTEGER LIST(50), the odd elements only;
    c) CHARACTER*10 TITLES(20), two elements to a line;
    d) DOUBLE PRECISION POWER(10), five elements to a line;
    e) LOGICAL FLAGS(10), on one line;
    f) COMPLEX PLANE(5), on one line.

2. Write statements to output the state of a game of tic-tac-toe (noughts-and-crosses) to a unit designated by the variable NUNIT.

3. Write a program which reads an input record of up to 80 characters into an internal file and classifies it as a FORTRAN comment line, an initial line without a statement label, an initial line with a statement label or a continuation line.

4. Write separate list-directed input statements to fill each of the arrays of Exercise 1. For each statement write a sample first input record.

5. A direct access file is to contain a list of names and initials, to each of which there corresponds a telephone number. Write a program which opens a sequential file and a direct access file, and copies the list from the sequential file to the direct access file, closing it for use in another program.

Write a second program which reads an input record containing either a name or a telephone number (from a terminal if possible), and prints out the corresponding entry (or entries) in the direct access file if present, and an error message otherwise. Remember that names are as diverse as Wu, O'Hara and Trevington-Smythe, and that it is insulting for a computer program to corrupt or abbreviate people's names. The format of the telephone numbers should correspond to your local numbers, but the actual format used should be readily modifiable to another.

8 PORTABILITY

1. Introduction

FORTRAN is one of the few universal programming languages. For two decades it has dominated all others in the field of scientific, numerical and technical applications, and only now are some inroads into its position being made as simpler, more modern languages like PASCAL come into increasing use for smaller non-numerical applications. Its universality has been founded on the wide availability of FORTRAN compilers across all types of computer architectures, from minis up to the large, number-crunching super-computers, and this has helped enormously to further the exchange of FORTRAN programs. But there have been problems.

Many manufacturers have taken it upon themselves to introduce into their compilers *extensions* to the language. These fall into two broad classes: those which are a general extension of the power of the language such as new types of control structures (for example, the DO...WHILE of some compilers), and those which give access to some particular feature of the hardware of the computer for which the compiler was designed. An example of this is the non-standard data types, like the reduced precision INTEGER*2 allowed in many compilers running on byte-oriented computers. These extensions to the language mitigate against program *portability,* the ability to transfer programs from one computer system to another, with little or no change, and to obtain the same results to the required level of significance. Fortunately, many good, modern compilers contain an option to indicate all statements which do not conform to the standard, enabling any necessary modifications to be made before attempting to transport a program from its original computer to another.

A further barrier to portability is the standard itself, as it does not contain complete specifications of all parts of the language, as we have seen when discussing, for example, the collating sequences in Section 2.2. In addition, there are many areas where the standard sets no limits, for instance the maximum depth to which DO-loops can be nested. These two facts give compiler writers considerable leeway in the manner in which they can implement the language and, inevitably, these different implementations lead to difficulties when moving code between computers.

A final obstacle to portability is the different internal number representation of computers of differing word length or architecture. Where this has an immediate consequence, as in the case for real DO-loop parameters (see also Section 4.4), it will be dealt with in the following sections. The more general problems of computer arithmetic and loss of significance in numerical calculations will not be covered here, but the interested reader is strongly urged to consult other specialised texts on this subject. It is all too easy to believe results just because they have been calculated by an 'infallible' machine, when in fact its inherent limitations have not been respected, and the results may be meaningless.

The increasing cost of producing and maintaining software means that the importance of writing portable programs is growing continuously, and this is, in particular, an essential requirement for libraries of subroutines intended for widespread use. Many scientific communities exchange programs amongst their members in a highly organized fashion. The need for conventions with regard to the portability of code then becomes evident, and the purpose of this chapter is to set out some basic rules which, if followed, will enhance portability. These points have often been touched upon in the foregoing chapters, but are summarised and augmented here for the sake of convenience.

The most basic rule is to adhere to the standard. This is not always as easy as it seems, as the standard is a long, formal document, which requires some expertise to interpret. It is often simpler to refer to a textbook based firmly on the standard (such as this one), or to one of those compiler manuals which carefully indicate which of the features described are standard, and which are not. The code, once written, can be checked for conformity to the standard by certain compilers, as mentioned above, using an option provided for this purpose.

Ingrained habits, however, die hard, and since many programmers have only ever learnt one particular dialect of FORTRAN, it is often difficult to persuade them of the value of restricting themselves to a subset of the dialect that they know. That is, nevertheless, the aim of this chapter. It lists certain rules which are often nothing more than a statement that a certain widespread practice is, in fact, contrary to the standard and will consequently degrade the portability of any program incorporating it. There are six sections, corresponding to Chapters 2 to 7 of this book, and those points which are considered to be very important for portable code are marked by an asterisk (*).

2. Language Elements

The rules given in this section concern the language elements covered in Chapter 2. Although breaches of these rules can cause difficulties, many of them can be repaired using editors or simple FORTRAN programs written for the purpose.

Character set

The standard defines a character set which contains upper case letters only. It is inadmissible to use lower case letters, except in comment lines, where indeed they are more readable:

    *   This is a comment line

There are thirteen special characters

$$\text{blank} \quad , \quad . \quad ' \quad : \quad = \quad + \quad - \quad * \quad / \quad (\quad) \quad \$$$

and no others should be used, even in comment lines, as they may not be representable on another processor (computer system).

Source form *

The standard defines a rigid source form: columns 1 to 5 for the label, column 6 for the continuation mark, columns 7 to 72 for the statement. This form should be respected, even though some compilers allow free form source.

Continuation lines

The standard prohibits the presence of any non-blank characters in columns 1 to 5 of a continuation line. Some compilers do not enforce the standard, but as there is no advantage in using this field, it should always be blank.

Multiple statements *

Some compilers allow more than one statement to be written on a line, separated usually by the non-standard semi-colon (;). This is not only non-portable, but bad style.

In-line comments *

Some compilers allow comments to be added to statements on the same line, usually following a non-standard exclamation mark (!). This is, in fact, admirable style but totally non-portable. However, such comments may be stripped off and placed on a standard comment line by a very simple program.

Column 2 of comment lines

Some programs which manipulate FORTRAN source code assign a special significance to certain characters contained in column 2 of comment lines. Unless such a program is never used, column 2 of comment lines should be left blank, in order to avoid any potential confusion when source code is manipulated by such a program.

Long names *

Some compilers allow names to have more than six characters. This is also an improvement in style, but highly non-portable, and very difficult to modify should that ever become necessary.

Currency symbol *

The standard defines no particular role for the currency symbol ($) but some compilers allow it to be used as a character in names. This is ugly as well as non-portable.

Logical constants *

The logical constants are .TRUE. and .FALSE.. Some compilers allow abbreviations such as .T. and .F. which should never be used.

Character strings *

Character strings are delimited by apostrophes ('). No other character, in particular the non-standard double quotes ("), should be used for this purpose.

3. Expressions and Assignments

The points dealt with here concern some potential problems in writing expressions, some of which can be difficult to detect. Adhering to the advice given will help to avoid unexpected differences in results when moving from one computer to another.

Mixed mode relational expressions

The standard allows mixed-mode relational expressions, such as in

IF (A/B .NE. I − J) THEN

These should be avoided, as rounding errors in the computation of the real expression may cause an unexpected change in control. For instance, the value of A/B for A = 1000.0 and B = 10.0 may not be exactly 100.0, but differ slightly from the true value, being say 99.9999. If I = 101 and J = 1, then the expression will have the value true, even though the two operands have apparently the same values, 100.0 and 100 respectively. The test may, therefore, work correctly on one computer but not on another.

Tests on equality

In a similar vein, tests on equality or inequality involving floating-point operands should be avoided, as rounding errors may cause them sometimes to be correctly evaluated, and sometimes not. This can depend on the values involved, and the computer being used. An example of poor code is

IF (A*B .EQ. C/D) THEN

*Comparison of character strings ***

The partial collating .sequences of the FORTRAN characters were stated in Section 2.2. It is perfectly legitimate to use relational operations on pairs of character operands whose individual characters are from the same collating sequence, for example, for a character variable CH containing a value composed of only letters:

IF (CH .GE. 'IJ') THEN

On the other hand, it is not possible to write portable code when the operands contain individual characters which are from different partial collating sequences. In order to make such comparisons, the lexical intrinsic functions (see Appendix A) should be used. These refer to an ANSI standard collating sequence. The (unlikely) statement

IF (LLE(' = *3B', '9$4 + ,')) THEN

will give the same result on all computers.

*Subscript expressions ***

Many compilers allow the use of non-integer subscript expressions. The value of the expression is rounded according to the normal rules. The use of such expressions can once again give results which vary from computer to computer because of rounding errors. If an expression is inherently real, it should be rounded explicitly to the *nearest* integer value, using the NINT intrinsic function, as in

A(NINT(P/Q)) = 0.

Even if P/Q evaluates to, say, 9.99999 this will still refer to A(10) as presumably expected.

*Number of subscripts ***

The number of subscripts in an array reference should be identical to the number of dimensions of the array, as specified in the array declaration:

```
INTEGER  I(10,10)
    :
K  =  I(3,4)
```

and not

```
K  =  I(33)
```

4. Control Statements

This section contains a few miscellaneous points refering to practices which are difficult to correct once the code is written, and which should therefore be avoided from the outset.

DO-loop parameters *

As we have seen in Section 4.4, there are potential dangers in using real quantities as DO-loop indices and parameters, both in evaluating the number of interactions and in the successive values of the loop index. Integer quantities should always be used for these purposes.

Arrays in nested loops

Nested loops should, preferentially, be arranged such that subscripted array elements are referenced in a manner allowing their first subscript to depend on the innermost loop and their last on the outermost loop, *e.g.*

```
    DO 1 J = 1,64
       DO 2 I = 1,64
          A(I,J)  =  B(I,J) + C(I,J)
  2     CONTINUE
  1 CONTINUE
```

Arranging loops in this way can avoid unexpected and dramatic losses in efficiency, connected with the way that words are stored in main memory (see Section 11.2).

Loop constructs *

Many compilers allow the use of non-standard loop constructs, such as DO...WHILE and DO...UNTIL. These should never be used.

*Branches into control constructs **

Some compilers allow control to be passed into the range of an IF-block or ELSE-clause, from outside its range. This is bad style, as well as being non-portable.

5. Specification Statements

This section has only four points, as most of the rules concerning specification statements are related to the specifications defined in connection with program units, and are dealt with in the next section.

*Data types **

The standard defines six data types – INTEGER, REAL, DOUBLE PRECISION, COMPLEX, LOGICAL and CHARACTER. No other data types should be used, nor should non-standard declarations, such as INTEGER*4, be employed where a standard declaration has an identical meaning (in this case INTEGER).

Some compilers allow variable initialization to be combined with type declarations in one statement. This is non-standard and should be avoided.

EQUIVALENCE statement

The use of the EQUIVALENCE statement for variables of different types can lead to problems if explicit use is being made of the internal number representations of a given computer. These may be different on another computer, and the code is thus non-portable.

*PARAMETER statement **

Some compilers allow intrinsic function calls to be placed in constant expressions in PARAMETER statements. This is non-standard, and should never be done.

*DATA statements **

No program should rely on the implicit data initialization of a specific operating system, for instance setting all variables not defined in DATA statements to zero. All variables which require initialization should appear explicitly in DATA statements, or in assignment statements.

6. Program Units

In this section we shall be concerned with program units and the specification statements which are relevant to them.

*Main program header line *

All complete programs must contain a main program. The optional header line of the main program, if present, must have the form

        PROGRAM name

and, in particular, should contain no parameter list. This list is sometimes allowed as a means of defining the I/O files that the program will use. Such files should always be defined in OPEN statements.

Intrinsic functions

A list of the standard intrinsic functions is given in Appendix A. No other intrinsic functions, as often provided by individual systems, should be used, as they are unlikely to be available elsewhere, and will have to be written explicitly.

Character to integer conversion

The values returned by the intrinsic functions CHAR and ICHAR are processor-dependent, and no portable program should depend on any specific values.

External functions

In order to satisfy a reference to a function not declared as external, a processor is permitted to supply any function known to it. To avoid surprises, portable programs must declare all external functions as such in EXTERNAL statements.

Side-effects *

Although allowed by. the standard, function subprograms should not alter the value of any of their arguments, nor of any COMMON variables, nor perform I/O, nor have any other side-effect. The order in which such side-effects are executed can be compiler-dependent, and can lead to different results on different computers.

COMMON variables as arguments *

Similarly, no COMMON variable should be passed as an argument if the COMMON block containing it is referenced in both the calling and the called subprogram, and the argument appears on the left-hand side of an assignment statement in the called subprogram or can be changed there in any other way.

Character variables in COMMON blocks *

The standard does not define any mapping of character variables onto computer words (or, as it describes it, between character storage units and numeric storage units – see Section 7.2). Although many compilers allow character variables to be mingled with other data types in COMMON blocks, no portable program should take advantage of this possibility as other compilers do not permit it. The relative positions of variables within a block could anyway shift, even if it is permitted, as the ratio of the size of a numeric storage unit to the size of a character storage unit varies from computer to computer.

Double-word data types in COMMON blocks

Some compilers require that those data types which require two storage units, COMPLEX and DOUBLE PRECISION, should be positioned so as to begin on an odd word in memory. Such variables should always be declared at the beginning of any COMMON block in which they appear, in order to ensure that this is always the case. If they appear anywhere else in the block, there may be an odd number of words between the beginning of the block and the variable(s) and they will then be mis-aligned for those compilers.

Names *

Although some compilers allow the duplication, no COMMON block name should be the same as the name of any subprogram.

Order of statements *

Although many compilers impose lax rules in this respect, portable programs should always observe the order of statements defined in Fig. 7 of Section 6.11.

SAVE statement

The SAVE statement should be used where appropriate, as this might be required on some processors on which the code will later have to run.

BLOCK DATA *

Where DATA statements are used for the initialization of COMMON variables, a BLOCK DATA subroutine should be used. The method by which BLOCK DATA is loaded is operating system dependent, and must be understood when installing programs on a given processor.

7. Input/Output

This section contains a number of points, which are mainly a recapitulation of points made in Chapter 7, but which are not always strictly observed by many compilers.

PRINT and READ statements

The PRINT and READ statements without a unit specifier cause I/O to be directed to or from processor-defined units. They should not be used in portable code, which should contain WRITE and READ statements with unit specifiers. These should be variables or symbolic constants whose values can easily be changed when transporting a program, if necessary.

*Non-standard I/O *

There are many non-standard I/O statements (for example, ENCODE/DECODE, DEFINE FILE, NAMELIST, PUNCH and asynchronous I/O statements). None of these should appear in portable programs, nor should any non-standard parameters be used in I/O statements.

Parameter lists

READ and WRITE statements may have either positional or keyword parameters. The two styles should not be mixed in one statement.

I/O file names

It is often convenient to reference files in OPEN statements by their unit numbers rather than their file names, as these are less compatible.

I/O unit numbers

I/O unit numbers should never be explicit constants or an asterisk, but rather symbolic constants or variables which may be readily changed when moving code from one computer to another.

*Format specification storage *

Format specifications may be stored in arrays. These arrays should always be of type character, although this is not required by all compilers.

Format specification separators

Although not required by all compilers, format specifiers in a format specification should always be separated by a comma (or by another legal separator such as a colon or a slash).

*IOSTAT parameter *

The values returned by the IOSTAT parameters in I/O statements are processor-dependent if an error occurs. No explicit use of specific numerical values should be made.

8. Summary

This chapter has consisted mainly of a list of rules restricting the the use of FORTRAN to somewhat less than the full language, and in any case to never *more* than the full language. To achieve a high level of portability, it is essential that any tempting extensions to FORTRAN are never used or if, for some overriding reason such as efficiency, they are used, that their use is clearly indicated and where possible an alternative standard FORTRAN version provided. Writing programs which are portable as well as correct is a skill which has to be learnt just like any other, and the increasing cost of software expertise, and hence of program conversion, makes it a highly desirable one to acquire.

9 FORTRAN STYLE

1. Introduction

The previous chapter dealt with the rather practical matter of portability, the advantages of which can be appreciated whenever a program, written to a sound set of rules, has been transported with little adaptation or trouble to another computer system. This chapter, on the other hand, deals with a more abstract question, the one of *style*. Style has no immediate effect whatsoever on the results or performance of a program; it is much less tangible but in the long-term just as important.

There was a time when most programs were fairly short, perhaps a few hundred or at the most a few thousand lines of code, and they were often written and used by one and the same person. This is no longer true. Today's FORTRAN programs can reach several hundred thousand lines of code, be written by a team of tens of programmers, have a lifetime of 20 years, and be read and maintained in the course of that lifetime by scores of other programmers. It is during the testing and maintenance periods of the so-called software *life-cycle* that the advantages of style become apparent (see Chapter 10). By making a program easier to read, and hence to understand, one eases the task of all those who must later carry out modifications, or look for errors in the code. It is possible to write code in such a contorted and opaque way, that no one but the author (and later not even the author) can understand it. In a worst case, code might be so difficult to grapple with that it is economically sounder, and more reliable, to write it again from scratch.

The purpose of this chapter is to lay down some ground-rules on style in FORTRAN coding. Like the previous chapter it contains a section corresponding to each of the Chapters 2 to 7 of this book.

The points listed concern coding at the subprogram level; those points which are more relevant to complete program design and style appear in the next chapter. If the recommendations listed here are followed, it is to be expected that the resulting code will be more readable, and therefore easier to test, modify and maintain, making it simpler to accommodate any changes in the specifications, algorithms or operating environment. Once again, they restrict the use of the language, but only in the same way as style in natural language makes it more disciplined, and hence more comprehensible. A final section points towards the problems of upwards compatibility with the next FORTRAN standard.

The practice of indicating the more important rules by an asterisk is again followed.

2. Language Elements

The points in this section concern the basic elements of the language, and programs which do not conform to them can often be brought up to standard by a utility program specially written for that purpose.

Comment lines

The FORTRAN standard allows comment lines to be inserted between continuation lines, and between program units. The first possibility can be useful if the comment is truly related to the continuation line which follows, but can be confusing otherwise, as it artificially separates the components of the statement. A further danger is that if the program is manipulated by a utility program of the type just mentioned, the source lines may be reformatted in such a way that any correspondence between the comment and the continuation lines may anyway be lost.

Comment lines between program units are easy to overlook, as they may be separated in compiler listings from the subprogram to which they refer. They should always appear inside the program unit to which they belong. Comment lines containing some sort of global information, can be enclosed between a subprogram header line and an END statement, thus making a clumsy but useful comment subprogram.

*Mnemonic names *

The names chosen for FORTRAN entities should convey some meaning. These are known as *mnemonic* names. It is far better to call, for instance, a variable WEIGHT rather than W or, worse still, PQ1. Using mnemonic names is one of the most important rules for coding, and we shall see in the next chapter how naming conventions can help circumvent the obvious limitation of a maximum of six characters for a name.

Split names

Since FORTRAN names are by necessity so short, there is never any need to make them still more difficult to read by splitting them across two lines of a statement. Similarly, names should not be typed with embedded blanks, as this makes them difficult to locate using an editor or other software tool.

*Initial lines *

A statement may consist of an initial line followed by one or more continuation lines. In this case, no line but the last should appear to terminate the statement legally. For example, all statements but the last should end in an operator or comma. In this way it is obvious, when only part of the statement is visible, for instance as the bottom line on a terminal display, that more of the statement follows.

Comment line symbol

The fact that code is written in FORTRAN 77, rather than according to a previous standard, is made immediately evident if an asterisk (*) is used in column 1 of comment lines.

*FORTRAN keywords *

FORTRAN has no reserved words, that is words whose use is restricted to a particular function in the language, and which may not be used for any other purpose. It is thus legitimate, but very confusing to write statements like

```
PARAMETER (IF = 10), (DO = 3)
REAL OPEN(IF), ENDIF(IF), REAL(IF)
```

This practice should be avoided.

*Use of blanks *

The appearance of code can be improved enormously by a sensible use of blanks to separate syntactic elements, for example on either side of equal signs, separators and operators. Compare

IF(SQRT(X**2 + Z**2).LT.A + 4.)PART(I + 3) = QUOT(4)

with

IF (SQRT(X**2 + Z**2) .LT. A + 4.) PART(I + 3) = QUOT(4)

*Order of statement labels *

In Chapter 4, certain control structures were recommended because, among other reasons, they tend to reduce the number of disturbing statement labels in a program. It is a great help in following the control flow of a section of code if the statement numbers in each program unit are in strictly increasing order. When coding, it is a good practice to start labelling with the number 10, and to increase each subsequent label number by 10. This leaves gaps in the numbering for later modifications. FORMAT statement labels should have a separate number series, say 1000, 1010, *etc.*

*Position of statement labels *

The visibility of statement labels is increased by positioning them to the right in the label field. Labels starting in column 1 tend to be obscured by the comment line symbol.

3. Expressions and Assignments.

This section contains only two points, concerned with the way in which assignments and expressions are coded.

Array subscripts *

It is possible to write subscript expressions deliberately in such a way that one or more of the individual subscripts is outside the range of the declared dimension, but that the array element thus referenced is nevertheless within the overall range of the array. For instance, with an array declared as A(10,5), a reference A(11,2) will exceed the range of the first dimension, but will correspond to the valid element A(1,3). This confusing type of practice should never be used.

Mixed-mode expressions and assignments *

The readability of mixed-mode expressions and assignments can often be improved by using explicit references to the relevant conversion functions (Appendix A). Compare

$$I = A + B/C$$

with

$$I = INT(A + B/C)$$

in which the conversion and consequent truncation are more evident without the loss of any efficiency.

4. Control Structures

The FORTRAN control structures should be used in a way that allows a reader to follow easily the logic of a program. The following points should be given special attention.

DO-loops *

Each DO-loop should terminate on a CONTINUE statement, and in nested loops each loop should have its own terminal CONTINUE statement. This is of great help when it is necessary to modify code by inserting branches to the label at the end of a loop.

   The structure of the loops can be made more apparent if their bodies are indented. This is particularly true for nested loops. A program to reformat source code in this way is given in Appendix B of Metcalf (1982). This point is demonstrated by comparing Exs. 21 and 22.

```
      DO 14 I1 = 1,N
      MAIN = N+1-I1
      LPIV = INDEX(MAIN)
      IF (LPIV.EQ.MAIN) GO TO 14
      ICOL = (LPIV-1)*IDIM+1
      JCOL = ICOL+NMIN1
      IPIVC = (MAIN-1)*IDIM+1-ICOL
      DO 13 I2 = ICOL,JCOL
      I3 = I2+IPIVC
      SWAP = A(I2)
      A(I2) = A(I3)
      A(I3) = SWAP
   13 CONTINUE
   14 CONTINUE
      DETERM = DETER
```

Example 21

```
      DO 14 I1 = 1,N
         MAIN = N+1-I1
         LPIV = INDEX(MAIN)
         IF (LPIV.EQ.MAIN) GO TO 14
         ICOL = (LPIV-1)*IDIM+1
         JCOL = ICOL+NMIN1
         IPIVC = (MAIN-1)*IDIM+1-ICOL
         DO 13 I2 = ICOL,JCOL
            I3 = I2+IPIVC
            SWAP = A(I2)
            A(I2) = A(I3)
            A(I3) = SWAP
   13    CONTINUE
   14 CONTINUE
         DETERM = DETER
```

Example 22

Block-IF

The block-IF is more understandable and therefore stylistically
superior to arithmetic- and logical-IF statements, and should be used
in preference to them. The block structure is made more apparent
if, as in the case of DO-loops, the clauses are indented (see previous
point) as shown in Exs. 23 and 24.

```
    IF (LINE(:1) .EQ. 'C' .OR. LINE(:1) .EQ. '*' .OR.
+    LINE(:1) .EQ. ' ') THEN
    IF (KNTCOM .EQ. KKLIM) THEN
    WRITE (NOUT, '(A72)') (CBUF(72*L5 – 71:72*L5),
+    L5 = 1, KNTCOM) , LINE
    KNTCOM = 0
    ELSEIF (SYNERR .OR. .NOT.STAT) THEN
    WRITE (NOUT , '(A72)') LINE
    ELSE
    KNTCOM = KNTCOM + 1
    CBUF(72*KNTCOM – 71:72*KNTCOM) = LINE
    ENDIF
    GO TO 2
    ENDIF
```

Example 23

```
    IF (LINE(:1) .EQ. 'C' .OR. LINE(:1) .EQ. '*' .OR.
+    LINE(:1) .EQ. ' ') THEN
       IF (KNTCOM .EQ. KKLIM) THEN
          WRITE (NOUT, '(A72)')
+             (CBUF(72*L5 – 71:72*L5), L5 = 1, KNTCOM),
+             LINE
          KNTCOM = 0
       ELSEIF (SYNERR .OR. .NOT.STAT) THEN
          WRITE (NOUT , '(A72)') LINE
       ELSE
          KNTCOM = KNTCOM + 1
          CBUF(72*KNTCOM – 71:72*KNTCOM) = LINE
       ENDIF
       GO TO 2
    ENDIF
```

Example 24

STOP statement

The STOP statement is unnecessary in a well structured program, as control should always be passed back to the main program, in which the END acts as a STOP.

RETURN statement

The simple RETURN statement is also unnecessary in a clearly written subprogram, as control can be passed back to the calling subprogram by executing the END statement. (It is possible to branch to the END statement, if necessary.) The alternate RETURN, on the other hand, is very useful for dealing with special conditions.

Backward branches

The use of backward branches is a severe impediment to program readability. They should be avoided wherever possible. Often they can be replaced by a DO-loop, and this is to be preferred.

5. Specification Statements

As in the previous chapter, most of the points concerning specifications are better dealt with in the context of program units. A few remaining items are covered in this section.

Default data types *

In order to permit an immediate recognition of the type of integer and real variables, constants and functions, their default data type should never be overridden. An expression such as

    I = A/B

is very confusing if I has been declared to be type real, and A and B type integer.

DIMENSION statement

It is preferable to use explicit type declarations for arrays, rather than the DIMENSION statement, *e.g.*

    REAL A(100),B(10)

rather than

    DIMENSION A(100),B(10)

Symbolic constants *

As much use as possible should be made of symbolic constants defined in PARAMETER statements. These permit easier program modification, and provide greater protection against inadvertent overwriting.

Mixed-mode initialization *

It is normally not a good practice to initialize a variable of one type with a value of another type. An exception is when a single-precision variable is initialized with a double-precision value; this allows the real variable to be promoted to double-precision during a later program modification, without having to change the initialization statement itself.

EQUIVALENCE statements

If EQUIVALENCE statements have to be used, they should be grouped with the array or other declarations concerned, in order to make the equivalence obvious.

DATA statements

For ease of readability, DATA statements should appear after all other specification statements and before any statement function and executable statements.

6. Program Units

Many points discussed in this section concern the use and layout of program units, especially with respect to their arguments lists and specification statements. It is important when reading code to be able to grasp quickly the meaning of all the declarative statements, as without the information they contain it is impossible to understand the executable statements.

Highlighting statement functions

Statement functions are unfamiliar to many programmers, and might be taken for the first executable statement of a subprogram. To avoid this happening, they should be enclosed between comment lines which make their purpose clear.

Formal parameters of statement functions

In order to avoid confusion, the names of the formal parameters of statement functions should not be used elsewhere as names in the same subprogram.

ENTRY statement

Although it is possible to use an ENTRY statement in a function subprogram, this is not good practice as it may conflict with the use of functions solely as functions in the mathematical sense, where a single value is returned, depending only on the arguments and with no side-effects.

*END statement *

As mentioned earlier, a subprogram should contain a single statement through which control is returned to the calling subprogram. This should be the END statement. If necessary, the END statement may be labelled and other statements may branch to that label. This ensures that there is no hidden return of control elsewhere in the subroutine.

In order to identify a particular label as representing a return of control throughout a whole program, all labelled END statements should bear the same label, for instance 999. It is then obvious that a statement such as

IF (VALUE. GT. TOP) GO TO 999

implies a return.

Alternate RETURN

Excessive use of the alternate RETURN feature can lead to a messy logic flow between subprograms. Its use should be reserved solely for exception handling *i.e* to deal with exceptional conditions or errors which are not normally expected to occur (arguments out of range, end of file on input, *etc.)*

External functions *

A list of the standard intrinsic functions is given in Appendix A. It is most confusing if external functions are written which have the same name as any of these, as the appearance of an intrinsic function name reference should always imply an actual reference to that function, and not to some other user supplied function.

Declarations of variables and arrays

It is helpful if variables and arrays are consistently declared in the following order:

  i) those appearing as formal (dummy) arguments, in the subprogram header line;

 ii) COMMON block declarations;

iii) those used only locally in the subprogram itself.

Arrays in COMMON blocks *

In order to make its nature clear, an array which appears in a COMMON block should have its dimensions declared in that COMMON block, and not in a separate DIMENSION or type statement.

Simple COMMON declarations *

In order to make COMMON declarations simpler, a single COMMON statement should define only one COMMON block. Similarly, a COMMON block should be completely defined in a single COMMON statement.

COMMON block names *

The name of a COMMON block should not occur elsewhere as a name in any subprogram in which it is referenced.

COMMON block definitions *

It is of the utmost importance that each declaration of a named COMMON block throughout a complete program should be identical in all respects. Failure to observe this rule can lead to program errors, as well as to difficulty in understanding the code (see also subsection 10.3.5).

Order of COMMON blocks *

It is easier to find one's way around the COMMON block definitions of a subprogram if the blocks appear in alphanumerical order.

Order of arguments *

The arguments in an argument list should normally be ordered according to their intended use: for input only, for output only, for input and output, as control variables, as external names, as an alternate RETURN. An example is

```
    SUBROUTINE CONVRT (VARIN, VAROUT, VINOUT,
+   NSTEP, FUNC, *)
```

Asterisk notation

If the extent of the last dimension of an array passed as an argument is unknown to the called subroutine, it should be declared using an asterisk (*) rather than with an artificially chosen value:

```
    FUNCTION MAXVAL (I)
    :
    INTEGER I(*)
```

Similarly, if the length of a character variable passed as an argument is unknown to the called routine, it too should be declared using an asterisk:

```
    SUBROUTINE GRAPH (CHAR)
    :
    CHARACTER* (*) CHAR (*)
```

Order of subprograms *

It is easier to locate individual subprograms in a listing or load-map if they are ordered alphanumerically within the complete program, following the main program.

7. Input/Output

The few miscellaneous points in this section are concerned with the use of I/O statements, helping to improve the robustness and appearance of code.

Error recovery

It is recommended to include the error recovery parameters ERR =, END = and IOSTAT = in all I/O statements on external files. This will ensure that the program will not fail during execution when an error condition arises.

PRINT statement

The PRINT statement writes to a default file whose unit number cannot be changed, nor does it allow any error recovery. It is preferable to use WRITE statements rather than PRINT.

FORMAT statements

FORMAT statements are often ugly in appearance, and spoil the look of well laid out code. It is better that they be grouped together, preferably at the end of each subprogram. They should also have a statement label numbering sequence independent of that used for the executable statements, for instance labels which are 100 times the label which is nearest to the statement first referencing the FORMAT statement:

```
     20 WRITE (NUNIT,2000) LIST
        :
   2000 FORMAT (1X,(A))
        END
```

8. Future FORTRAN

As has been mentioned in Chapter 1, there is likely to be a new standard for FORTRAN introduced at the end of the decade, currently called FORTRAN 8x. This standard will classify certain features presently in FORTRAN 77 as *obsolescent*, and these will be candidates for eventual removal from the language. Certain other features become redundant with the introduction of FORTRAN 8x (Metcalf and Reid, 1987). Long-lived code can achieve a large measure of upward compatibility by avoiding the use of such features in new FORTRAN 77 programs wherever possible. Some of them are, however, currently essential; those which are not are listed below.

i) The arithmetic-IF (use the logical or block-IF, as appropriate).

ii) Branching to an ENDIF statement (branch to the following statement).

iii) The computed GO TO (use a block-IF).

iv) The alternate RETURN (use a user defined flag).

v) DO-loop parameters of type real (code the loop with integer parameters), and DO termination statements which are shared or which are not CONTINUE statements.

vi) The DIMENSION statement (use the appropriate type statements instead).

vii) The little used ASSIGN and assigned GO TO statements.

viii) The PAUSE statement, (use an appropriate READ statement).

9. Summary

This chapter has presented in a systematic and summary form a list of points which, if adhered to, will enhance the appearance and hence readability and maintainability of FORTRAN programs. As with the recommendations on portability in the previous chapter, the effect is to restrict the great freedom allowed by the FORTRAN standard, but the long-term benefits to be gained from following a set of conventions are so great that the initial extra effort in coding is paid back over and over again during the lifetime of the code.

10 DESIGN OF FORTRAN PROGRAMS

1. Software Engineering

In the early days of computing, a customary method of writing a program was to think a little about the problem, maybe to sketch a flow-chart, then to take a coding sheet, or even rush to a key-punch, and make a first attempt at writing the code. This code would contain only those features for which there was an immediate need, generalisations, special cases and comments would then, of course, be 'added later'. The longest phase of the programming effort was occupied by 'debugging' − stumbling line by line, error by error, through all the many defects in the code, some of which would require major changes in the program, as they were the result of 'logical errors' (illogical thought) during the initial phases. This has been described as coding in haste and debugging at leisure.

Nowadays everything is, or should be, quite different. Today we proceed in a manner determined by thoughts about 'life-cycles', 'top-down design', 'data structures' and so on (see below), spending much of the programming effort in thinking about what has to be done and how to achieve it, before spending relatively little time writing code. This code, once freed of a few typing errors, works quickly on all the carefully prepared test cases. More realistically, that is a goal towards which we can at least strive, and the purpose of this and the following chapters is to summarize a few conventions, oriented mainly towards large FORTRAN programs, and which, if followed, will assist in the production of software which is relatively:

− free of design errors;

- rapid to test;

- easy to understand;

- straightforward to modify;

- unlikely to require complete rewriting;

- robust;

- efficient;

- well documented.

The general principles are also applicable to small programs.

The benefits to be derived from this approach can be very great. The whole of the design and implementation becomes planned and methodical, increasing productivity and eliminating wasted effort caused by misunderstandings, duplication or false starts. It is clearly far cheaper to correct a basic design error whilst still in a program design phase, than if the error is first detected only during program testing.

The final product is one which is easier to use and maintain, so that the further benefit of user productivity is obtained. It is now well known that the maintenance phase of a large program can dominate all others in terms of cost, and it is therefore of the utmost importance to ease the task of those involved in maintenance by a sound initial design and comprehensive documentation. The overall better use of resources which this approach is likely to engender can bring with it a better utilisation of computer system resources.

The fact that the whole project is properly planned just as when building, for instance, a bridge, has led to this discipline being termed *software engineering*.

This chapter begins by considering the initial design of a program, and continues by emphasizing the way in which certain FORTRAN language features should or should not be used. The importance of documentation will be stressed.

2. Program Design

Modern programs are often so large, and deal with such complex inputs and outputs, that it is no longer possible, nor even desirable, for one person to be responsible for a piece of software from its inception through to its last run. The need to work in teams in an effective manner imposes the need for a *methodology*, or formalised way of proceeding through the various phases of the *life-cycle* of the code:

i) user requirements (what the users want the software to do, in their terms);

ii) definition of software requirements (how the users' requirements translate into a feasible program or suite of programs);

iii) specification of the program (definition of each function that the program must perform);

iv) detailed design of the program (a translation of the specification into the design of modules, subroutines, data structures, algorithms, interfaces, *etc.*);

v) coding of the program;

vi) program testing;

vii) program use;

viii) program maintenance, (often the longest in time for the programmers involved).

There exist many methods for tackling these phases, some of them quite formal, and an excellent exposition has been given by Freeman and Wasserman (1980) and by Yourdon (1983). In those cases where an informal method is opted for, it is nevertheless important to have agreement among the participants — the design team, coding team, maintenance team and the final users — about the results of each phase. This can only be achieved if there are comprehensive written documents available which can be reviewed by everyone concerned. If there is disagreement about what a piece of software is supposed to do, there is little point in discussing the possible ways of doing it.

Table 4

Items to be defined for software requirements

1. *Introduction*

General statement of the purpose of the software, those participating in the design, and the time-scale.

2. *List of documents used in the definition of the requirements.*

3. *General description*

3.1 Function and purpose.

3.2 Environmental considerations (which compilers and operating systems are to be used, what hardware constraints *etc.* exist).

3.3 Contrast with previous projects of a similar nature, pointing out especially why different circumstances require different design choices.

3.4 Relationship to current projects of a similar nature, pointing out especially how the projects may collaborate.

3.5 General constraints (for instance, the total time allowed, or the distributed nature of the programming over many sites).

4. *Specific Requirements*

4.1 Functional requirements (hardware-software trade-offs, redundancy, error handling, operator or user considerations).

4.2 Performance requirements (speed, processing rates, response times etc.).

4.3 Interface requirements (to other software, or to hardware).

4.4 Operational requirements (including the user or operator interface).

4.5 Resource requirements (memory, peripherals etc.).

4.6 Testing requirements (which tests are essential for the final acceptance).

4.7 Documentation requirements (to support the software).

4.8 Quality requirements (those particular to the project, *e.g.* algorithm efficiency or precision).

The plea then of this section is to write down at each stage of the design a list of critical points which can be discussed and debated. The *user requirements* are usually taken for granted, and often in FORTRAN environments the designers, implementors and users are one and the same group, but it is nevertheless by working on a definition of requirements that basic differences about the objectives of the project can be resolved very early and at little cost.

A document to be agreed upon at the end of the second phase, the *definition of software requirements,* might cover the points given in Table 4, which are based on standards used by ESA (1982).

Once these points have been agreed upon (or even before, in most cases), it is possible to begin to design the *architecture* of the software corresponding to these requirements. The major part of this task is to decide on the data structures, and on the decomposition of the program into *modules*, or groups of subprograms performing specific functions on defined sets of data, and to describe the function of each one together with its place in the control logic and flow of data. The document produced at this *program specification stage*, still assuming informal methods only are applied, might cover the points listed in Table 5 (again based on ESA standards).

This document, once agreed, allows the *detailed design* of the program(s) to proceed. Choices have to be made on the auxiliary systems *(e.g.* program libraries and utility packages) to be used in the final implementation, and detailed specifications of each part of the system must be provided, sufficient to allow the coding to be carried out fairly easily. This assumes that the algorithms to be used are obvious. This is clearly not always the case for new programs, but by defining appropriate data structures combined with a good modular structure, it is often straightforward to compare one algorithm with another in the same test-bed. In practical terms, the documents resulting from this fourth phase would contain:

i) definitions of the data structures (layout of arrays and COMMON blocks);

ii) definitions of the input and output of each module;

iii) definitions of the algorithms for transforming the input data into the output data.

Following straight on is the *coding phase* which should proceed according to agreed conventions, such as:

i) the coding conventions defined in Chapters 8 and 9;

ii) rules for defining constants (see Section 3.5 below);

iii) rules for common sections of code (see Section 3.6 below);

iv) rules for in-line comments (and/or documentation, see Section 12.5);

v) naming conventions for program units, files, local variables, COMMON blocks, COMMON variables, *etc;*

vi) procedures for distributing work;

vii) a procedure for integrating code into master source code libraries.

Especially in situations where the programming is carried out by a large or dispersed team on a variety of computers it is vital that agreed conventions and rules be adopted and applied. Only in this way can inevitable overheads of communication between the participants be kept to a minimum.

The final phases of producing efficient code and of testing and maintenance will be dealt with in the following chapters.

Table 5

Items to be defined for program specification

1. *Service information*

1.1 Abstract.

1.2 Table of contents.

1.3 Procedures for updating the document.

1.4 Log of updates to the document.

1.5 List of reference documents.

1.6 Control procedures.

2. *Software description.*

2.1 Decomposition into modules.

2.2 Functional definition of the modules (input, output, response to control variables).

2.3 Description of the control flow (of the modules).

2.4 Description of the data flow (through the modules).

2.5 Definition of the control structure.

2.6 Definition of the data structures (including the information read and written by each module).

2.7 Test definition for each module.

3. *Development plan*

3.1 Breakdown of work into convenient parts.

3.2 Association of work with teams of people.

3.3 Schedules and milestones which must be achieved.

3.4 Critical issues (for instance availability of computer time and of tools).

3.5 Manpower estimates.

3. Good Programming Practice

This section is concerned with good style in the use of the FORTRAN programming language, and as such it deals with its large-scale features rather than with the small-scale ones of coding covered in the two previous chapters.

3.1 Data structures

A precise definition of the data structures used within a program is widely regarded as the most fundamental aspect of the overall design. Unfortunately, the present FORTRAN standard supports only very primitive data structures — arrays and COMMON blocks — as part of the language. Users who require more advanced structures, such as linked lists, trees, heaps *etc.*, or PASCAL style records, have to program them themselves. (For examples of algorithms see, for instance, Aho *et al.*, 1974).

The fact that these structures cannot be based on protected data types, such as a pointer data type, means that they are always susceptible to inadvertent overwriting, but this problem can at least be partly overcome by writing packages to support the structures, and allowing access to them only through function and subroutine calls, while never exposing the structures openly in COMMON blocks which could be accessed elsewhere in the program. Early design of the data structures, even if only in terms of COMMON blocks, is vital to a successful design of the whole program structure.

3.2 Program structure

Programs should have a modular structure. There are many ideas about how this can be achieved, but in practice one can adopt a *top-down* approach and proceed by an increasingly fine definition of the tasks of the modules, until one arrives at a definition for each module which corresponds to a task which can, typically, be written in a few pages or less of FORTRAN. Thus, a program may consist of high-level modules for initialization, processing and termination, and each of these may be progressively broken down (refined) into smaller units, observing two fundamental rules:

– to minimise module *coupling* (interconnection between modules);

– to maximise module *strength* (the internal communication within a module).

At some time during this process, it will become clear that there are functions which are required in many parts of the program. These should be coded as library functions or subroutines, ensuring that they are kept in one place only, for ease of testing and modification. If existing libraries are to be used, this has to be taken into account earlier in the definition of the program structure, the top-down approach then being combined with a *bottom – up* design, a situation which is common in practice.

The choice of whether a given task is performed by a function or subroutine should normally be based on the principle that functions should return a single value as a function of its arguments, and have no other side-effects. All other tasks should be coded as subroutines. At the same time, functions should not be written with an excessive number of arguments, as the risk of making coding errors grows as the number of arguments increases.

The way in which the modules are designed is intimately linked with the program data and control structures, which have to be designed at the same time. In the final description of each module one needs to provide documentation giving information on its interfaces to other modules: under which circumstances and how it is called, which data it has available to it, which data it should generate or modify and how, in turn, it calls other modules. In this way the data themselves structure the program.

In this context an attempt to 'hide' certain data structures should be made, as mentioned above. Mechanisms for doing this are not truly part of the FORTRAN language but the desired effect can be achieved by providing packages of routines for servicing certain data structures. For instance, rather than making all the coded details of the description of a machine under design open to (erroneous) modification and use, it might be better to hide the details in a package which alone has access to the structure, and which will provide any required details *via* a subroutine or function call. This is true even if some penalty with respect to run-time efficiency is incurred. This cost will be recuperated in programmer efficiency during the life-cycle of the software. The principal I/O of a program should always be performed *via* packages of this type, especially as these help with portability.

This modular approach will have significant advantages in the testing phase, as each module can be tested individually before incorporation into the final program.

3.3 Program libraries

As mentioned in the previous subsection, it is during the design of the program structure that decisions can be made about which external libraries of subprograms to use. Here it is as well to be sure to select those libraries and programs which are well supported and kept up-to-date, avoiding especially subprograms which are likely to become obsolete in the anticipated life-time of the software being coded. It might also be appropriate to re-use code from existing programs, but only if it is of an acceptable standard. If it is not, it is better to re-code the algorithm, rather than to spoil a new program with bad code. One is helped here if there are automatic tools to improve the layout of code, but these do not help if it is fundamentally badly structured.

3.4 Procedure calls

During the program design consideration needs to be given to whether arguments rather than COMMON blocks should be used for passing data between subprograms. In general, arguments should be used if the quantities involved are passed only through one level of reference, and especially so if they represent the arguments of a function, or take advantage of FORTRAN's ability to handle variably dimensioned arrays. In other cases, COMMON variables are to be preferred (but the rules given in the next subsection should be observed).

3.5 Declarations

The readability of a program is improved enormously if each subprogram begins with a clear set of declarations. These should be laid out neatly, and be well commented. The following specific points should be followed:

i) COMMON block definitions should be stored in a single place, and referenced using a mechanism such as the INCLUDE statements of some compilers. (This statement is a non-standard method of inserting sequences of lines from a named file, but this point is of such importance that it is better to use INCLUDE statements, and to generate standard code to transport to another computer if necessary, than to run the risk of using different definitions in different subprograms).

ii) Each COMMON block should contain variables which are logically associated.

iii) A subprogram should not contain COMMON blocks which are not required in that subprogram.

iv) The dimensions of COMMON arrays should be in the COMMON declarations themselves, and should be defined as often as possible in terms of symbolic constants defined in PARAMETER statements:

```
PARAMETER (NPTS = 20)
COMMON /POINT/ YPTS(NPTS),ZPTS(NPTS),....
```

The PARAMETER statements should be accessed also from a single place using a method such as the INCLUDE statement. Those which are linked to COMMON arrays should be stored with the COMMON block in question. The same applies to any explanatory comment lines.

It is most useful if all COMMON variables follow a single naming convention, if only one as simple as that they should always have six characters (and other variables fewer than six characters). This permits a ready visual identification of the scope of variables when reading the body of the code, *i.e.* whether a variable is local to a subprogram or global to a whole program. Other more sophisticated conventions may be developed as appropriate, for instance fixing the last letter of all COMMON variables to be Q or X or some other character. In addition, one-line descriptions of all COMMON variables should be maintained, for instance in a dummy subroutine of comments.

DATA statements should be used only to initialize variables. All constants should be defined in PARAMETER statements. They may be propagated through a program as parts of standard sequences using the INCLUDE or similar mechanism. In no case should constants be defined in assignment rather than PARAMETER statements, nor should they be buried inside expressions.

Finally, the EQUIVALENCE statement should be avoided as

much as possible, especially if used only to save space. This 'saving' can become costly later in the life-cycle when obscure overwriting errors are being sought. For the same reason, a single variable name should never be used for two different purposes.

3.6 Expressions

A strength of FORTRAN is the way that it permits mathematical expressions to be directly transcribed into code. This facility should be used sensibly, and the following points should be observed:

i) expressions should be written clearly, avoiding tricks and unnecessary variables:

$$DISCR = SQRT (B**2 - 4.*A*C)$$

and not

$$B2 = B*B$$
$$AC4 = 4.*A*C$$
$$DISCR = SQRT(B2 - AC4)$$

ii) however, several simple statements should be used in place of a single complicated one if clarity is improved;

iii) blocks of common code should be structured as functions, subroutines, or as statement functions, rather than being repeated in several places;

3.7 Control Structures

The theory of structured programming tells us that all programs may be built using only three constructs – a straight sequence of code, an iteration with only one point of entry and one point of exit, and a selection between several paths based on a condition. In FORTRAN the iteration can be achieved by use of the DO-loop, although the **for**-loop, DO..WHILE and DO..UNTIL constructs of other languages are considered to be better structured in this respect. The selection can be achieved using the IF..THEN..ELSE structure. On the other hand, the overuse of the following constructs or features will lead to code which is badly structured compared to code which uses them sparingly:

   i) branches, especially backward ones (loops should be used instead);

   ii) complicated loops (they should be kept simple, with only one exit);

   iii) long subprograms (they should be kept short, performing only one clear function);

   iv) names which are misleading or convey no meaning;

   v) names which are so similar as to be confusing (particular care must be taken with names containing the pairs of characters 0 and O, 1 and I, 2 and Z, 5 and S);

   vi) tricky programming (especially if not commented);

   vii) over-complicated statements;

   viii) non-indented loop bodies and IF-clauses.

Well structured code reads top-down, and this helps greatly with the initial testing and later with readability and maintenance.

3.8 I/O Statements

In a well structured program the input and output will be localized in an I/O package. However, that deals only with the physical transfer of data, and two further problems remain: data verification and the handling of the specific I/O for steering the program and checking its results.

The following points on data verification should be observed:

   i) test that data are valid, plausible and consistent, in other words that they represent correct values, ones which are reasonable within the context of the program, and that they are not only individually correct but also compatible with one another;

   ii) in particular, before using an input item as an array subscript, format specifier, argument to a function, DO-loop parameter or in any similar circumstances, it should be checked to be within range;

iii) try to recover from data verification errors if they are isolated, but terminate the program if they become too frequent;

iv) deal with parity errors as with bad data;

v) deal with end-of-file conditions by correctly terminating the program; input data should always terminate on an end-of-file or some standard mark, rather than relying on a counter.

With respect to any data records read by a program for steering purpose, it is simpler either to use a single standard format for all the input data, or to use the list directed I/O facility of FORTRAN 77. Different formats for different records can be a significant source of errors when using a program.

Input data of this type should always be copied to an output file for later verification or checks. Where larger amounts are concerned, at least some identification of the data which have been read should be given in an understandable message. Long, complicated sequences of input data records can often be avoided by an appropriate choice of default conditions under which the program should run. These should correspond to what is considered to be the normal mode of operation of the program, and deviations from this normal mode should be selected when required, rather than adopting the opposite approach in which every tiny detail of the program operation has to be specified by each user (cf. IBM's JCL which has no defaults, and requires every single detail to be specified).

During a program run, there should be enough summary output printed in clear formats for the user to be able to understand what operations the program has performed. Should there be a specific need for more detail, this should be obtainable by optional switches activated by the user by means of input data records (or by user commands if working interactively rather than in batch mode). Such switches should provide, in a general case, several levels of information selected on a module-by-module basis, such that the user can probe the inner workings of the program without having to recompile with his own WRITE statements. The information should be clearly formatted, and its point of origin within the program should be obvious.

The program should terminate with a summary of the whole run, which should provide on a single page for later filing sufficient details of the run for it to be reproduced at a later date.

4. Summary

The discipline of software engineering is of great importance in providing tools and methodologies which enable large software projects to be managed in a safe and efficient way. At the level of the design of large FORTRAN programs there are some valuable lessons to be learnt, even if no formal methods are actually employed. This chapter has drawn together some of the relevant points which should be borne in mind from the very beginning of such an undertaking, and which should go a long way to ensuring its successful outcome.

11 PROGRAM EFFICIENCY

1. Preliminaries

Among computer scientists there is a widely held opinion that program efficiency is one of the least important aspects of programming. The argument runs that other aspects such as clarity of code, portability of programs and minimum investment of manpower are more relevant; in those cases where program run times become too long or computers overloaded, it is economically sounder to increase the hardware capacity than to expend a large effort in tuning the software. This attitude ignores not only the plight of programmers struggling daily to maintain tight schedules on inadequate or overloaded computers, but also the fact that sometimes dramatic improvements in program execution speeds can be achieved with relatively little effort.

The purpose of this chapter is to set out a list of guidelines to efficient coding which will help to ensure that reasonably fast code is written from the outset. The same guidelines can also be applied to existing code, but this book is more concerned with the concepts required to learn effective coding, than with first-aid measures to be adopted with old programs.

Writing an efficient program proceeds in three steps:

i) selection of the most efficient algorithm consistent with other requirements such as accuracy, stability and robustness;

ii) consideration for efficiency during the coding, but without detriment to other factors such as clarity of the code and portability;

iii) a final check on the presence of 'hot-spots' - areas of the code taking too much time to execute − and their elimination if possible.

In no case should the effort invested in the last step exceed the likely return in savings of computer time.

It is possible to make only very general remarks about algorithm selection. It is assumed here that programmers working in specific areas, whether they be scientific, commercial or educational, will be aware of the existing body of experience in their particular field, and will take that into account when developing algorithms for new programs. Before designing new algorithms it can be effective to look around amongst the work of colleagues, or in program libraries or in specialist publications. Only when such a search proves to be fruitless should one begin to design a new algorithm, and then textbooks can be of great help in providing the basic methods.

When writing the actual code, it is indeed true that an attempt to write well optimized code straight off can be an obstacle to the production of programs which are of high-quality in terms of their structure, and of the other attributes such as clarity mentioned above. At this stage it is necessary only to avoid practices which are clearly inefficient, and to concentrate on developing a well structured and laid-out program which is understandable and which will be portable and robust *i.e.* work well for many different types of input data. In this way the code will have a potentially long life and will be useful also to others. Only when writing very large programs or library programs which will be heavily used does it become necessary to devise code which is efficient from the outset, at least in those sections of the program which, on the basis of experience or calculation, can be shown even before the program is run to be potential hot-spots. In these cases it may be useful to test several different algorithms before making a final choice.

When a fully working and tested program is finally ready, it is as well to make a check on the presence of hot-spots. There exist many methods for performing this investigation, but they are all dependent on the local operating system being used. The best ones are profiling tools which show which proportion of the total CPU-time of a program is spent in each of its subroutines, or some other program sub-division. A badly optimized program will typically be characterized by a few large peaks in this time distribution, and the final task is then to attempt to eliminate these peaks in order to produce a flatter distribution for a shorter total run-time. It is important here to know when to stop. Normally the most dramatic improvements are made quickly, and subsequent ones become successively more difficult and less effective, unless whole algorithms are replaced by faster ones.

One important aspect of program efficiency is the type of compiler used, and which of its optimization options, if any, is selected. It is assumed in this chapter that the source code is compiled using an optimizing compiler at its highest level of optimization. This is often quite sufficient to achieve a high degree of efficiency without any further modifications to the code, as modern compilers are usually able to deal with coding practices which formerly would have severely degraded performance.

The rest of this chapter is organized such that those points which are normally the most important appear towards the beginning. Since DO-loops present a particular problem they are dealt with first in a separate section. The material is presented summarily, and the reader who wishes to have more details and background information is referred to Metcalf (1982), which is a comprehensive treatment of the whole topic.

2. DO-loops

The DO-loop is one of the most frequently used constructs in FORTRAN. It is clear that the code within a DO-loop will normally be executed more frequently than the code outside, and the deeper the level of nesting the more this is true. (We ignore here special cases such as loops which have a zero trip under typical running conditions, being executed only in particular circumstances). For this reason, improvements in the run time of programs are often achieved by modifying some of the DO-loops. These modifications can be detrimental to clarity, and should be carried out only on those loops which are proven to be responsible for significant fractions of the execution time. If nested loops are correctly nested (see below), there will normally be no need to modify any but the innermost loop.

External references

Modern compilers contain extensive procedures to optimize the code inside DO-loops, as compiler writers have obviously concentrated on this area for the reasons just stated. The degree to which a loop can be optimized depends on many factors, but particularly on its complexity in terms of the number and type of branches it contains. If the sequence of code is interrupted by many branches, especially backward ones, it is broken up into many small pieces, or *blocks,* whose inter-relations are difficult for the compiler to analyse and optimize. Most harm is done by branches to code outside the loop, and the most difficult of these for the compiler to handle is a reference to an external subprogram. This is true whether the reference is executed or not. The compiler cannot know whether, in a statement such as

IF (FLAG) PRINT*, ' VAR1 ',VAR1

the logical condition will be true or false at execution time, and the external reference implied by the I/O statement will inhibit complete loop optimization, as the compiler will assume that a reference will actually be made and will generate additional instructions to prepare for the call, even if at execution time the call is not made.

For the usual references to functions and subroutines the compiler must assume that all global variables − those in COMMON blocks and the argument list − might be modified by the called subprogram, and will take action to store any such values which are in registers before the call, and to retrieve them after the call. These instructions are in addition to those generated for the call itself and constitute an additional overhead.

The ability to structure programs using subprograms is one of the most important structuring features in FORTRAN, and it is therefore only with some reluctance that DO-loops should be modified to remove external references. Where this must nevertheless be done, there are a number of actions which are possible:

i) If the DO-loop containing an external reference is fairly short, it might prove effective to *push* the loop into the called subroutine. In that case the body of the loop will then consist of the whole of the subroutine, and a better degree of optimization might be obtained.

ii) If the external subroutine is fairly short, it might prove effective to *pull* the whole of the subroutine into the loop. Once again, the loop becomes larger, and may result in a better overall optimization.

iii) If the external reference is to a short function subprogram, it might be possible to rewrite it as a statement function in the calling subprogram. Statement functions normally give rise to the generation of so-called *in-line code, i.e.* the instructions required to execute the function reference are expanded in the place of the reference, and no branch to the function is necessary.

iv) If the external reference is to a larger function subprogram, it might be rewritten directly as in-line code.

All the practices just described are undesirable in well-structured programs, and should be employed only where absolutely necessary. However, in all cases they certainly save the overhead of the subprogram calls.

Loop nesting

Each DO-loop consists of three parts — an initialization, a body and a termination. The initialization and termination constitute an overhead. For a loop which has M iterations, the initialization will be executed once and the termination M times. If the loop has nested inside it another loop having N iterations, the initialization of the inner loop will be executed M times and the termination M*N times. The total number of initializations is then $M+1$, and the total number of terminations is $M+M*N$, or $M*(N+1)$. Taking two values of M and N which are different in magnitude, say $M=100$ and $N=2$, the two totals will be 101 and 300, respectively. Here a loop with only a few iterations is nested inside a loop with many. If the order of nesting were reversed, the two totals would be only 3 and 202 respectively, bringing an evident saving in the loop overheads. For this reason loops should always be nested in this manner, with the highest number of iterations in the innermost loop, if the problem allows it.

Array subscripts in nested loops

In the loop

```
      REAL  A(20,5),  B(20,5),  C(20,5)
      :
      DO 2 I  =  1,20
         DO 1 J  =  1,5
            C(I,J)  =  A(I,J)  +  B(I,J)
    1    CONTINUE
    2 CONTINUE
```

two arrays are added together and stored in a third. In most modern compilers, the subscript expression for the position of each array element in the array, $20*(J-1)+I$, which contains a multiplication, will be replaced by an equivalent initial value of I to which 20 is *added* each time J is incremented. If the subscripts were written in the reverse order, *i.e.* if the array were processed in column order rather than row order, the subscript calculation $20*(I-1)+J$ would be replaced by an equivalent initial value of J to which 1 would be added each time I is incremented. Normally it is of little consequence whether the arrays are processed in column order or in row order, as in neither case is any multiplication carried out. However, in some exceptional circumstances the order of array subscripts can have a dramatic effect on efficiency:

i) This can happen when the arrays are very large, and stepping across the rows implies accessing array elements which are widely dispersed in the various levels of storage, which can lead to serious loss of efficiency in accessing the array elements. Stepping down the columns implies accessing contiguous elements in store which is more efficient.

ii) Most main memories are organised in *banks,* and successive words in an array are stored in successive banks and not contiguously in one bank. This means that if contiguous elements of an array are referenced each bank is addressed in turn. If the elements are addressed by row, and if the length of the columns in the array (in the appropriate storage units) is an exact multiple of the number of banks in memory, then only one memory bank will be referenced, leading to a severe loss of speed of transfer of the data words to the CPU

iii) The last reason for preferring to address the elements of an array by column is that the increment of 1 at each iteration is often faster to perform than an increment by column length, 20 in our example, either because it corresponds to a machine instruction, or because the value 1 is more likely to be kept by a compiler in a register, as it is a more commonly used constant.

It is interesting to note that the order of subscripting can affect efficiency in different ways on different computers, for instance because the number of memory banks varies from machine to machine, and what happens to be efficient on one machine can be inefficient on another, just because the column length of an array happens to be the same as number of memory banks.

Conformable arrays

In the example of a DO-loop just given we note that each of the three arrays has the same column length, and so the compiler can generate code to compute subscript addresses just once and use them for all three array references. This would not be possible if the column length differed, and it is therefore a good practice to use arrays of the same length in all but their last dimension, if they are used with common subscript references in DO-loops of this type. This implies that some arrays have to be overdimensioned, an example of efficiency costing space.

Loop unrolling

We have seen above that there are overheads associated with the execution of a DO-loop. For very short loops these overheads can be just as costly as the execution of the body of the loop, and if in addition there are very few iterations, just two or three, it can be advantageous to eliminate the loop completely by writing out the body explicitly, thereby saving the overheads.

For short loops with a larger or indeterminate number of iterations, the number of iterations can be reduced and the length of the body increased by *unrolling* the loop. In

```
    DO 1 I = 1, 100
       A(I) = B(I) + 4.
  1 CONTINUE
```

the loop overhead is comparable to the cost of the loop body. If it is rewritten as

```
    DO 1 I = 2,100,2
       A(I - 1) = B(I - 1) + 4.
       A(I) = B(I) + 4.
  1 CONTINUE
```

then the number of iterations is halved for the same total number of operations inside the loop. This can be an effective technique in short, inner loops. Attention must, however, be paid to end effects if the loop is unrolled to a degree which is not an exact divisor of the number of iterations, for instance in the example above if the number of iterations were odd rather than even.

Invariant code

It often happens that a DO-loop contains expressions or sub-expressions which do not depend on the loop index. For instance, in

```
REAL SCALE(10), RADIUS(20)
:
DO 1 I = 1, N
    VOL(I) = 4./3. * PI * SCALE(J) * RADIUS(I)**3
1 CONTINUE
```

the sub-expression 4./3.*PI.*SCALE(J) remains unaltered, or *invariant* during the execution of the loop. As long as this is obvious to the compiler it will generate code to evaluate the sub-expression just once outside the loop, and use this computed value inside the loop. A modern, optimizing compiler will normally perform this task more efficiently than if a programmer defines and uses a temporary variable for the same purpose. The only condition is that the expression be written in the form shown in the example, with the constant terms followed by invariant terms followed by terms which depend on the loop index. For any other order there is no guarantee that the constant and invariant terms will be recognized as such.

3. General Techniques

The techniques described in this section are equally applicable to code inside or outside DO-loops. Clearly they will be more effective when used on code inside DO-loops, but their effectiveness in no way depends on the properties of the loops themselves.

Eliminating functions

In the last section we learnt of the importance of removing function calls from critical loops, in order to improve loop optimization. In many cases functions represent a considerable proportion of the time spent in program execution, and the program can be speeded up by eliminating the functions completely, rather than by just moving their code around. For instance, suppose it is necessary to make a test as to whether a point is inside a sphere centered at the origin of the coordinate system. The test might be written

$$\text{IF (SQRT(X**2 + Y**2 + Z**2) .LT. RADIUS) THEN}$$

involving a reference to the costly SQRT function. Such a test is better written as

$$\text{IF (X**2 + Y**2 + Z**2 .LT. RADIUS**2) THEN}$$

which is equivalent, but involves no function reference. Similar improvements can be made in the case of the trigonometric functions.

Another powerful technique to eliminate functions is to replace them by predefined look-up tables. Such a table will contain the values of the function at representative points, and depending on its size and nature can be set up in a DATA statement or calculated in a separate part of the program written for that purpose. A large, costly table might even be calculated once and for all by a separate program, stored on a permanent file and be read in by any program which requires access to it. If a function value is required at a point which lies between two of the points in the table, it can be calculated by a suitable interpolation method.

Constant sub-expressions

In the previous section we met the invariant sub-expression 4./3.*PI*SCALE(J). Supposing that PI had been defined as a symbolic constant in a PARAMETER statement, the sub-expression 4./3.*PI would then be a *constant sub-expression* and would normally be evaluated by the compiler at compile time, and this value substituted for the constant sub-expression. In order to help the compiler identify constant sub-expressions, it is essential that all the constants and symbolic constants be grouped together, and not separated by non-constant terms, as would be the case in 4./3.*SCALE(J)*PI.

Common sub-expressions

Within a short section of code a certain sub-expression may appear several times. If none of the terms of the sub-expression is changed between the various references, such a sub-expression is known as a *common sub-expression*. An example is

```
X = A - B + 4.*Y
Z = A - B + 2.
```

in which $A - B$ can be identified as a common sub-expression. Such sub-expressions can occur in a single statement:

$$X = (A - B)*Y - Z + (A - B)/3.$$

In both cases a modern compiler is capable of identifying the statements as containing common sub-expressions, and will evaluate these only once. With some exceptions it is normally necessary to write the sub-expressions identically for each occurrence, and the use of parentheses is recommended to help with their identification. The exceptions are that some compilers will recognise A*B and B*A, or A + B and B + A, as being common.

Strength of operations

The various arithmetic operators, +, −, *, / and **, vary markedly in the speed at which they execute. The order beginning with the fastest is normally the one just given, but can vary from computer to computer and as a function of the types of the operands. For instance, a real value raised to an integer constant power will normally be evaluated faster than the same value raised to a real power. It is thus better to write A**3 rather than A**3.0. The important point is that an attempt should be made to reduce as much as possible the number of operations, and to prefer fast ones to slow ones. This is known as *strength reduction,* and can often be achieved by factorising expressions, as in the case of

$$W = X*(S + T) + Y*(S + T) - Z*(S + T)$$

which can be written with fewer and faster operations as

$$W = (X + Y - Z) * (S + T)$$

even if the common sub-expression had been recognised by the compiler and evaluated only once.

Mixed mode expressions and assignments

FORTRAN allows a great degree of freedom in writing expressions and assignments containing terms of different types, for example

    $I = A/J$

where the variables are of their default type. This freedom can be the source of a significant amount of inefficiency, as the compiler has to generate a large number of extra instructions to change the variables from one type to another. In the example just given the code generated would be equivalent to

    $I = INT(A/FLOAT(J))$

whereby J is first converted to type real and the quotient back to type integer, two quite lengthy processes as the number representations for these two data types are quite different, as we have seen in Section 7.2.

    It is a good practice to keep the number of such conversions to an absolute minimum by choosing the types of the variables carefully, and by grouping variables of a given type together in sub-expressions whenever possible, as in

    $A = I*B*J*C*K*D$

which is written more efficiently as

    $A = (I*J*K) * (B*C*D)$

EQUIVALENCE statement

The use of the EQUIVALENCE statement is not only associated with poor style, but can also often lead to a degradation in efficiency. By joining sets of variables together in so-called *equivalence classes*, the compiler tends to become confused about storage association, and inhibits some of its optimization procedures. For instance, in

    COMMON /TEST/ A(10),S,B(10)
    DIMENSION C(20)
    EQUIVALENCE (A,C)

```
      :
X  =  A(I)
S  =  0.
Y  =  A(I)
```

the entire contents of /TEST/ usually become bound into a single class. The compiler cannot optimize the two fetches of A(I) into a single fetch, for fear that its value is changed between the two references by the assignment to S.

In general it is poor practice to equivalence loop indices and parameters, or scalar variables to array elements, or to equivalence together variables of different types.

Unformatted I/O

We have seen in Chapter 7 that there are two formatting styles for I/O lists, formatted and unformatted. Unless the data in the I/O lists are to be displayed for reading by the human eye, (or possibly by a different computer), it is far better to use unformatted I/O statements. A formatted statement involves a conversion between the internal number representation and the character string of the external representation, and this leads to a considerable drop in efficiency. Not only that, but there is usually a loss of precision on output, and if the data are stored on a medium such as a disc file they will normally occupy more space as well.

I/O lists

An I/O statement usually causes a minimum of three calls to be made to the I/O system routines, one to initiate the data transfer, one to perform the data transfer and one to terminate the data transfer. Depending on the nature of the I/O list additional calls will be necessary for the data transfer, possibly one for each item on the list. It is thus more efficient to consolidate lists into a single array, either directly or via an EQUIVALENCE statement (a rare example of it enhancing rather than degrading efficiency).

Particular attention should be given to the way in which arrays are referenced in I/O lists. Whereas

WRITE (NUNIT) A

or

WRITE (NUNIT) (A(I) = 1,100)

will normally give rise to the minimum of three calls to the I/O
routines, lists of non-contiguous elements such as contained in

WRITE (NUNIT) (A(I), I = 1,99,2)

or

WRITE (NUNIT) ((B(I,J), J = 1,100), I = 1,100)

will result in a call being made for *every* array element in the list.
To increase efficiency in such cases it is preferable to copy the
required elements to a temporary array, and to output them with a
single reference to that array. A similar strategy can be adopted for
input.

FORMAT statements

When formatted I/O is used, some improvement in the inevitable
overhead involved can be gained by ensuring that the format specifications are available to the compiler at compile-time, enabling it to
decode them and to prepare the I/O instructions in an optimal way.
This means that the specifications should be given either directly in
the I/O statement − explicitly or as a symbolic character constant
− or as a reference to a FORMAT statement, for example

PRINT '(A/(6F10.3))', 'LIST OF TEMPERATURES', TEMP

What should be avoided is the use of character variables or expressions as format specifiers, as these can be decoded only at execution-time. The specifications themselves should be kept as simple and
as short as possible.

CHARACTER data type

This particular paragraph is intended more as a word of warning
than as a general statement. The introduction of the CHARACTER
data type into FORTRAN was viewed in different ways by different
vendors. Some considered that it would be little used in FORTRAN
programs, and felt justified in implementing it inefficiently, carrying
out each operation or assignment of a character variable by a reference to system routines. This means that code involving the

CHARACTER data type can be very slow. On the other hand, some vendors have implemented this data type using efficient machine language instructions, and the corresponding object code is fast. No general statement is possible, it is simply necessary to find out which type of implementation is available on the computer being used, and to judge whether or not overall program efficiency is likely to be compromised.

Whatever the type of implementation, the concatenation operator is inherently slow, and should be used as sparingly as possible.

IF statements

The most important general comment about IF-statements is that the order of testing of compound relational expressions should reflect the likelihood of the individual expressions being true or false. In the sequence

```
IF (MARK.EQ.10) GO TO 10
IF (MARK.EQ.23) GO TO 20
IF (MARK.EQ.35) GO TO 30
IF (MARK.EQ.41) GO TO 40
```

it would be important, if the value of MARK were normally 41, to make that particular test first rather than last, in order to save the usually redundant tests against the other values. This is equally true for a sequence of ELSEIF tests in an IF...THEN...ELSE construct.

A similar situation holds for single logical IF statements containing a series of .OR. or .AND. operators. In statements like

```
IF ( L.EQ.1. OR. M.EQ.2. OR. N.NE.3 ) GO TO 10
```

and

```
IF ( I.EQ.10 .AND. J.EQ.20 .AND. K.EQ.30 ) GO TO 20
```

it is important to allow the compiler to generate object code which breaks off the sequence of tests as soon as an individual test is fulfilled or fails, respectively. Thus in these two examples, L being equal to 1 should be the most likely condition, and I being equal to 10 should be the least likely condition, respectively. If this is not the case the expressions should be rearranged accordingly.

The arithmetic IF statement is normally slower, as well as less understandable, than the logical IF statement. Where it is nonetheless used, it is faster to follow the statement immediately with the statement bearing the label of the first of the three branches:

IF $(I - J)$ 10,20,30
10   ......

Use of COMMON variables or argument lists

In FORTRAN there is a choice of the method by which values of variables and arrays may be communicated between two subprograms. There may be valid reasons of program design to choose between the one method or the other as shown in Section 10.3, but as far as efficiency is concerned the faster method is usually to use COMMON blocks rather than argument lists. This results from the fact that the values of COMMON variables are stored and fetched by direct references to their addresses, whereas for argument lists the addresses are usually stored as some form of table which has to be constructed, and which is referenced indirectly through a pointer. This represents an additional overhead, although the difference is often not very great nowadays.

Initialization of variables

Most programs make use of constants and variables which have to be defined before program execution can begin. There are three principal methods by which such initialization may be carried out:

i) The PARAMETER statement, which should be used for all true constants. The symbolic constants thus defined will be used by the compiler as a normal constant in any optimization procedure, for instance in the evaluation of constant expressions at compile-time.

ii) The DATA statement, which should be used for all variables requiring an initial value. It should not be used, however, for variables which do not require an initial value, for instance by unnecessarily setting all variables in a program to zero. This can disguise coding errors which would otherwise be revealed during execution, especially on systems which set uninitialized variables to a special out-of-range value.

iii) The assignment statement, which should be used only for repeated initialization of a variable, for instance at the beginning of each iteration of an iterative procedure. An assignment such as

    START = 4.362

used for initialization has the triple overhead of requiring firstly a location to store the constant of the right-hand side, secondly an instruction to perform the assignment, and thirdly the execution of a store to memory, which is an expensive operation.

Large tables of variables may be initialized by other methods of course, for example by reading them from backing store, by copying them from some other storage area, or by calculating their values. These are obviously more expensive procedures, and where necessary should be implemented according to the advice given on I/O earlier in this section.

4. Summary

Whether program efficiency is important or not depends totally on the context in which a program is to be run. Will it be run often, or for long periods? Is there ample computer time available? Will the cost of the extra effort involved outweigh the potential savings? The work involved in improving run-time performance can vary from a small investment yielding a spectacular improvement, to much effort giving virtually no change. The decision as to whether to attempt to improve a program should be made having regard for all the factors involved. For new programs, the application during coding of the efficiency rules outlined above will help to make later improvements unnecessary.

12 TESTING AND DOCUMENTATION

1. Introduction

In Chapter 10 the concept of the software life-cycle was introduced in the context of program design. This chapter continues that discussion into another of the phases of the life-cycle, that of program testing. For a small program, testing will involve ensuring that it produces correct output for prepared test cases. These should be designed to cover the various possible input values and conditions in such a way that there is a high degree of confidence in the program's correctness for the cases which have not been covered. For a large program, it will involve testing each module in a similar way, and then going on to ensure that the modules as a whole produce output which conforms to the written specifications.

It is possible, in fact usual, that a tested program will at some later stage fail to perform correctly in some unforeseen circumstances. The errors causing the program to fail in these circumstances are known as *bugs* and locating and correcting them as *debugging*. This procedure is clearly intimately linked with testing, as the more thoroughly a program is tested the fewer bugs it is likely to contain. Since it is also possible that the corrections made to remove a bug may perturb the program in other ways, debugging always has to be followed by testing again on representative data in order to ensure that this has not in fact happened. Testing and debugging are the main topics dealt with in this chapter, and the reader who wishes to pursue this study in greater depth than is possible here is referred to Myers (1979) for the general principles of software testing, and to Howden (1982) for some hints on testing scientific programs in particular.

The importance of documentation was also stressed in Chapter 10. Only by preparing carefully written and detailed specifications is it possible to eliminate many potential errors during the design phases and to have an agreed statement against which the program can be tested. Equally important during the program testing and maintenance phases is the availability of good in-line documentation and of written program manuals. Some advice on these topics will conclude this chapter.

2. Initial Module Testing

A program which performs a computation of any complexity will have an enormous number of combinations of different paths through it, depending on the various branch and control statements it contains as well as on the diversity of the input data it might be expected to handle. It is an impossible task to test each possible combination and every possible set of data, but initial program testing can be simplified by breaking the program down into reasonably sized components – subprograms and groups of subprograms (or modules, see Chapter 10) – and by setting up different sets of test data which exercise the components over the whole range of input with which they are supposed to deal. Testing by module reduces the number of possible paths through the code substantially: if a program with 64 possible paths through it can be divided into two modules each with eight paths, then the total number of paths to be tested is reduced to 16.

Modern FORTRAN compilers often contain aids to program testing, varying from informative cross-reference maps to powerful interactive debugging facilities. A first vital step in a major software undertaking is to ensure that the compiler and operating system which are to be used are adequate for the task, as great gains in productivity can be obtained by an initial appropriate choice of the compiler and the FORTRAN environment in general. In the rest of this section the use of a good compiler will be assumed; it contains a list of points to be observed at each stage of testing a subprogram or small module of subprograms.

2.1 Test compilation

The first step in testing a subprogram is to perform a test compilation. This does not simply mean trying to reach loading and execution with no fatal errors generated by the compiler, but actually checking that the compiler listing contains no error messages of any level of severity whatsoever. Most compilers now issue error messages graded according to the supposed gravity of the error, typically varying from informative through warning to fatal. The compiler messages should be checked to see whether they include any error message at all, as even what for the compiler is a trivial error can be the manifestation of a more serious problem.

Some compilers perform the inadmissible function of 'correcting' small errors of syntax. Such errors should be immediately attended to by the programmer for two reasons. Firstly, the compiler's action may not be correct in the context of the program and, secondly, it is undesirable to leave source code uncorrected for small errors which might then be considered as fatal by another compiler if the code is moved to another computer.

2.2 Cross-reference map

When all the compiler errors have been eliminated, a compilation listing with the fullest possible cross-reference map should be obtained. This should be examined carefully for any revealing information. For instance, in the list of variable names there may be variables which are mis-typed versions of other variables, and these typing errors should be corrected. Similar errors may be present in the list of external references. There may be statement labels which are marked as being unreferenced. This can happen either because they are genuinely unused, in which case they should be removed, or as the result of the mis-typing of a statement label reference which should then be corrected. There may also be statements marked as dead code because they cannot be reached, and this is certainly the result of a coding error which should be corrected. Many modern compilers give an indication when a local variable is either completely unused, or used on the right-hand side of a statement before it has been defined. This second condition is a very serious one and should be corrected immediately.

2.3 Desk-checking

As a last check before execution testing begins, it is useful to read the final version of the source code before continuing further – so-called desk-checking. It is often possible to pick up errors in the logic of the program by reading it through and trying to imagine how it will execute on simple data, and far faster than the same errors can be detected by repeated test executions. This is especially true if this desk-check is performed by a colleague, or at least in collaboration with a colleague to whom one tries to explain the program logic. More formal checks of this type are known as *walk-throughs*. During such a check the following common sources of error should be kept in mind and checked for:

i) each variable should be defined before it is used;

ii) each array subscript value should be within the declared bounds of the array;

iii) equivalencing of variables of different types may introduce incorrect use of a data type;

iv) all arrays should be correctly declared;

v) variables should not be initialized with a DATA statement when an assignment is intended (see Section 6.6);

vi) mixed-mode computations or comparisons should be properly understood;

vii) expressions should be so written that arithmetic underflows or overflows are not likely to occur;

viii) most divisions require a check on the divisor being zero, and the consequences of integer division must be understood;

ix) the rules of expression evaluation must be properly understood;

x) compound relational expressions require careful checking;

xi) DO-loops with non-constant parameters may potentially be infinite loops;

xii) arguments in calling and called subprograms should agree in number and type (and length for characters), and where applicable the same units for physical quantities should be used;

xiii) actual arguments which are constants should never be altered in a called subprogram;

xiv) files should be explicitly declared in OPEN statements with the appropriate attributes;

xv) format specifications should correspond to the I/O lists.

2.4 The first executions runs

After the successful completion of these first three steps, but not before, it is the moment to try to load and execute the program. If the list of external references has been properly checked as described above, the loading step should give no problem, unless there is a mis-match in the number or type of the arguments passed between subprograms. As loaders do not normally make a check for this discrepancy, it should be carried out by hand prior to the first load.

At this stage of testing the use of an interactive debugging compiler is highly recommended. The program should be executed without compiler optimization, but with full subscript and substring range checking, and with any other testing aids such as trace-back which may be available.

If the program fails to complete execution for any reason, then it is important to read carefully all the available information about the cause of the problem. A fatal execution error is often caused by a non-fatal error which has occurred somewhere previously during execution, and it is essential to extract all the relevant information about the error, and not just that associated with the actual program failure.

2.5 Boundary conditions

A frequent type of programming error is that a section of the code works correctly for most of its running conditions, but that it is incorrect at the extremes of the ranges involved. DO-loops may perform one too many or one too few iterations and arrays may be under-dimensioned by one. It is important to check for this type of error, as it may go undetected until the program is in use, and will be yet another bug to be found later.

2.6 Data checks

In a similar vein it is important to check the program over the whole range of its input data, especially at the extremes of the range. Equally important is to test the program's reaction to invalid data. The old programming adage 'garbage in, garbage out' is sheer nonsense, as any well designed program will test for meaningless or unacceptable data, and will respond by rejecting them and issuing an appropriate diagnostic message.

2.7 Non-standard features

Chapter 8 was concerned with guidance for enhancing program portability. An essential practice is the avoidance of non-standard FORTRAN features — those not specified by the ANSI standard. Good compilers indicate in their associated manuals which of the features they offer are non-standard, and by selecting an appropriate option this can often be checked by the compiler itself. This check should always be performed, and the appropriate remedial action taken.

2.8 Checking on another system

It is remarkable how often the presence of hitherto undetected errors is revealed by moving a program to another type of computer. It is wise to take advantage of this fact by installing a new program on at least two different types of computer just for this purpose. The two systems should differ as much as possible. Errors show up because of differences in initialization of memory, different compiler limits, better checking of program syntax and semantics, and the different order of loading. This last difference provides an especially good means for detecting hidden overwriting errors.

A further advantage of this type of check is that numerical programs may show themselves to be unstable with respect to a different number precision, and the necessary steps can be taken to improve the algorithms before the code is released.

This type of test run on another system is, of course, only worthwhile for a complete program rather than just a program module, and for large programs should be delayed until the testing stage of the whole program. This is the subject of the next section.

3. Initial Program Testing

This section is concerned not with the detailed testing of code, but rather with the way in which a complete program composed of individual modules should be tested and maintained. This testing will be carried out in conformance with the testing specifications which formed part of the program design, and clearly the overall results obtained from the program should correspond to those set out in the design documents. The design of test cases is a non-trivial exercise for large programs, particularly because of the large numbers of different types of input data they may have to deal with and the immense number of different paths through the code. Nevertheless, a set of representative data and a definition of their expected output form the basis of an essential first test, and more exacting cases can be dealt with once these basic ones have been covered.

A particularly intractable problem is to ensure that all possible paths through the program have been taken at least once. It is on untested paths that bugs will be lurking, waiting to reveal their presence when the code is finally put into production. One aid to demonstrating that each path has been exercised is the use of some form of profiling tool, as mentioned in the previous chapter.

The psychology of program testing is such that a programmer usually has an innate belief in the correctness of his own code, and will tend to subject it to less severe testing than it deserves, and to be less critical of unsatisfactory performance. For this reason it is an excellent principle that program testing be carried out by a different group of people from those who actually wrote the code. Independent testers are likely to be more demanding and more critical than the original authors, and will often take a more detached view, regarding the program in a different light.

Whoever performs the testing, it is most important that detailed logs of the various tests be maintained. These should include sufficient information on the input to be able to reproduce a test if necessary. The program output can often be stored in a computer file, which enables it to be more easily subjected to automatic checking or comparison. The test inputs should include invalid as well as valid data.

There is a rule, based on much experience, that errors in programs tend to cluster, and that the more errors that have been detected in a given section of code the more there are remaining to be found, compared with more reliable sections of code. This means that if a program contains one or two modules which are particularly troublesome compared with the rest of the program, there may come a point at which it will be considered to be more cost-effective and much safer to re-write those modules. This is, of course, a major decision as the module specification, coding and testing cycle will have to be repeated from scratch, but it will at least be done with the advantage of experience based on hindsight.

The time spent in testing rises with the complexity of the modules which comprise the program. In order to keep testing time to a reasonable length it is necessary to find a suitable compromise between module complexity and program complexity – the less complex the modules the more complex the program as there will be correspondingly more modules. A ground rule here is to avoid at the program design stage the specification of modules which are trivial, but to be alert to the problems of testing modules which are too complex, both individually and as part of a program. Module complexity is often measured in terms of what are taken to be significant parameters such as the number of variables and statement labels a module contains, as well as the depth of nesting of the code and the extent of the use of backward branches.

An important aspect of testing is the amount of time which is planned for it. It is a grave mistake to attempt to rush testing in order to deliver a piece of code in the shortest possible time. The overall costs involved, which being manpower-intensive are very heavy, are bound to rise as a result of such an approach, since the code will certainly not have been subjected to a sufficiently thorough and complete testing, and correspondingly more time will be spent, expensively, sorting out the bugs during the rest of the program's life.

Later during the life of a program, additional or replacement modules will often have to be incorporated into an already working version. This is an operation which has to be undertaken with great care, and is akin to the initial program testing discussed above. In this case, however, a few additional precautions are necessary in order to ensure that as well as working in its final environment, a new module has no deleterious effect on the rest of the program. Usually a replacement module should not only be tested against its specifications, but should also be demonstrated to be better than any previous version, for instance that its algorithms are more efficient, or that it is faster, smaller, more robust or more portable, or some desirable combination of these attributes. If the results from the new module are expected to be identical to those from the old, this comparison can often best be carried out by a comparison program, always provided that the results are written to an output file using identical formats or identical unformatted record structures.

Incorporating new modules into existing programs is a task which is usually best entrusted to someone acting as an administrator who then has the opportunity to become familiar with all the details of the program, and who is able to adopt a ruthless attitude towards new code, ensuring that it conforms to any standards and conventions which might have been agreed upon, as well as carrying out formal testing. An experienced person of this type will have the possibility to build up suites of test cases which in the course of time can include various 'pathological' cases which test the program to its absolute limits.

4. Debugging

As much as one tries to test a program thoroughly, programs of any appreciable size have such a large number of different paths and are able to deal with such varying inputs, that inevitably many combinations of these will not have been tested. When a combination which produces an erroneous result is encountered after the release of a program to its users, the presence of a bug is revealed. Bugs can manifest themselves in various ways – by a single incorrect result, by many wrong results from some point on in the execution of the program, or by the execution being prematurely terminated by the operating system.

The sources of bugs are numerous, some of the most common ones being listed earlier in Section 12.2. In the case of wrong results it is often easy enough to use an interactive debugger (or to insert print statements into the suspected area of code) in order to check which of the variables concerned has an unexpected value, and to trace back the fault to its source. A tricky problem in batch mode can arise when the insertion of a print statement causes the bug to disappear! This is usually a sign of overwriting, and the apparent disappearance of the bug is caused by a change in the position of the relevant variables in the loaded program, either because of the code generated by the the print statement itself, or because the subprogram containing the print statement is now loaded in a different position with respect to the other subprograms. As overwriting is one of the most difficult errors to find, one often has to resort to a patient trial of different print statements in various places, noting the apparently sensitive areas of the regions in which variables are stored, and continuing by intuition or inspired guesswork. Frequent causes of overwriting are loops which exceed their bounds, or the incorrect passing of an array dimension as an argument between two subprograms.

A program may crash for a variety of reasons which depend on the operating system and hardware being used. In many cases it is possible to recover from such errors, and to terminate the program gracefully, printing out some useful information which will help to identify the source of the error. Whereas older systems provided little more than a memory dump and possibly a trace-back of the sequence of calls, modern compilers often contain options which generate symbolic dumps which are annotated for easy comprehension by a programmer who is unfamiliar with assembly language. A disadvantage is sometimes the mass of information provided by such symbolic dump facilities, but there are usually means of controlling the quantity produced.

Common FORTRAN errors which cause crashes are:

  i) infinite loops leading to a time-limit being exceeded;

 ii) erroneous array subscripts causing a location outside the range of the program to be referenced;

iii) overwriting of code leading to an attempt to execute an illegal instruction;

 iv) on some systems, an attempt to use an uninitialized variable as an array subscript or as an operand in an arithmetic expression;

  v) division by zero;

 vi) generation or use of a value which is outside the allowed arithmetic range — an underflow or overflow.

A good operating system will provide, at least optionally, sufficient information for these bugs to be identified rapidly, and for corrective action to be taken. However, interactive debuggers are the most convenient means of bug detection, and should be used whenever available.

Detecting and correcting more intractable bugs is a demanding exercise requiring skill and experience. A useful technique for a difficult bug is to discuss it with colleagues who may have encountered similar ones in the past, or who might be able to suggest a fresh approach. It is important to ensure that all the information available has been carefully sifted for clues, noting any suspicious signs of program malfunctioning, and then constructing a series of tests which allows various hypotheses about the source of the error to be checked.

Once a bug is detected and located, the correction to be applied must be written and tested. Even changing a single line of code in a program can have ramifications far beyond those connected with the surrounding code, and it is therefore essential to ensure not only that any correction has removed the bug itself, but also to repeat relevant test cases in order to be certain that that no new bug has been introduced as a side-effect. Experience shows that corrective code is itself a significant source of new bugs, and great care must be taken to test it properly, although this requires some self-discipline in the hurried conditions which frequently accompany debugging.

5. Program Documentation

A program is of virtually no use whatsoever to others, and usually not even to its author, unless it is accompanied by proper documentation. Since this subject is of a general nature rather than being related to FORTRAN as such, it is dealt with in this section only briefly, but is mentioned because it is such such an essential part of any program. Nevertheless, in order to place documentation in a FORTRAN context the section is divided into three parts – the in-line documentation of a subprogram, the in-line documentation of a complete program, and user manuals. The purpose and implementation of each of these three types is different, as will be explained below. Further bibliographic references relevant to this topic are given by Gaggero (1983).

5.1 In-line subprogram documentation

A well designed program is composed of subprograms each of which performs a single, well defined task. The reader of such a subprogram may be looking for one of three different levels of information. The first level concerns the overall purpose of the subprogram, its inputs, outputs and the method it employs to transform the one into the other. Assuming the subprogram works and the reader is not interested in further details, this information is often all that is required. A full list of the points to be mentioned in such a case is given in Fig. 8.

Many of the points given in Fig. 8 are optional for a given subprogram, but none should be omitted if it is applicable. The information should be boxed with asterisks for two reasons, firstly to highlight the comments and secondly to provide a means whereby a simple program can extract such boxes from the rest of the source code, to be listed as a form of automatically generated printed documentation. The entry points to the subprogram are marked by a symbol different from that marking the other items in order that they can be picked out separately by such a listing program as an option.

Most modern computer systems permit a sample empty box to be stored on a file, which can then be copied into a new subprogram and filled in as necessary. A suitable interactive command language procedure could even prepare such boxes

```
***************************************************************
*     *SUBROUTINE RANNUM                                      *
*                                                             *
*     - LIBRARY CODE:      V123                               *
*                                                             *
*     - AUTHOR:            J. Smith                           *
*                                                             *
*     - DATES:             First release 15.06.83             *
*                          Last revision 17.09.84             *
*                          (author's bug fix)                 *
*     - DESCRIPTION:                                          *
*     Pseudo random number generator with normal             *
*     distribution, zero mean and unit variance.             *
*                                                             *
*     - METHOD:            See reference                      *
*                                                             *
*     - ARGUMENTS:         RANDOM (O/P) A pseudo              *
*                                     random number           *
*                                                             *
*     *ENTRY POINT:        NORRUT                             *
*     -    ARGUMENT:       SEED (O/P) Current value of        *
*                                     seed                    *
*                                                             *
*     *ENTRY POINT:        NORRIN                             *
*     -    ARGUMENT:       SEED (I/P) Replaces current        *
*                                     value of seed           *
*                                                             *
*     - EXPECTED INPUT:    None                               *
*                                                             *
*     - FINAL OUTPUT:      See argument descriptions          *
*                                                             *
*     - RESTRICTIONS:      None                               *
*                                                             *
*     - NON - STANDARD                                        *
*       FEATURES:          None                               *
*                                                             *
*     - FILES REFERENCED:  None                               *
*                                                             *
*     - REFERENCE:         J. Ahrens, Math. Comp., 27,        *
*                                     927 (1973)              *
***************************************************************
```

Fig. 8 The contents of a subprogram description box

automatically in a question-and-answer session.

The second level of subprogram documentation is that provided for a reader who wishes to acquire an overall understanding of the subprogram's structure and algorithms. This can be regarded as a type of paragraph heading in which the significance of blocks of code is described. Reading the second level comments from a subprogram should be sufficient to answer any questions concerning the methods, and to be able to locate a section of code performing a given sub-task. Such comments can be distinguished by spacing before and after the comment lines, and by using asterisks in columns two and three as well as well as in column one. An example is

```
***

***    SOLVE THE EQUATIONS OF MOTION
***
```

Comments at this level can also be extracted by program for listing as printed documentation, or be selected by an editor to view on a terminal screen without the associated code.

The third level of in-line documentation is the detailed comments on the actual FORTRAN code itself. Such comments should be brief but not trivial. They should convey information which is not immediately obvious from the code, and not merely reflect the statements. A poor example is

```
*

*    INCREMENT N
*

     N = N +1
```

A better example is

```
*

*    SEARCH FOR PIVOT ELEMENT
*
```

A mistake to avoid is the use of so many comment lines that the code itself becomes obscured and difficult to read, a real problem if it is displayed on a terminal screen of limited size. A good proportion is 25 to 30 per cent of the total number of lines, for the second and third levels combined. In general, the layout of the comments should be consistent throughout the subprogram, always using the same style and starting in the same column.

An important point is that the comments must be maintained to correspond with the code whenever the latter is changed to such an extent that the original comments no longer apply. Nothing is more misleading than comments and code which do not agree. Similarly, the comments contained in new code inserted into an existing subprogram should conform to the style for comments already used there.

Finally, the use of blank lines or lines of asterisks to separate blocks of code, and particularly the declarative statements from the executable statements, can be recommended.

5.2 In-line program documentation

A complete FORTRAN program may be only a few lines long or hundreds of thousands. This fact makes constructing general guidelines difficult, but nevertheless some points appropriate for medium-sized programs of some thousands of lines are given here, and authors of smaller or larger programs can adapt them to their needs.

Depending on the size of the program and the form in which it is stored and maintained, the program documentation can be concentrated into a single comment block preceding the main program, or be divided into blocks placed at appropriate points in the source code, perhaps in the form of comment subprograms.

The first requirements concern the program name, version number, date of the version and other maintenance log information. A list of authors should be provided, plus a short description and any references to the literature. An explanatory list of all the external files which are used must be given. To help a reader find his or her way around the code, a directory of subprogams is needed, showing any grouping into modules. A list of all common blocks is essential, together with a brief description of all variables and arrays in the common blocks. In the case of logical arrays, a finer breakdown into array elements may be required.

In some cases this header information might also include details of use, restrictions and so forth, but if this is voluminous it is better to provide it as a separate user manual. Proposals for these are given in the following subsection.

5.3 User manuals

A simple, short program might require only a single sheet of instructions on how it is to be used. More substantial programs will require more elaborate documentation, and in the limit three separate documents might be provided. The first of these is a simple guide for routine use of the program. This should be directed at users who are not necessarily specialists in programming, or even in the methods used by the program, but should enable them to manipulate the program easily, obtaining the desired output from the provided input. In general such a user guide will have six sections:

i) a summary of the purpose and use of the program, with any references;

ii) an outline description of the methods used, of the operation of each program module and of the different options available;

iii) a description of the inputs;

iv) a description of the corresponding outputs;

v) a list of error codes and a description of recovery procedures;

vi) sample jobs, including the job control language.

The second item of user documentation is intended for those who require a much more detailed description of how the program functions, and consists of a complete guide on a module-by-module basis to the whole program. It should include descriptions of test cases and timings, so that users have a basis for comparison when performing their own tests.

The third document required is a detailed description of all the input and output formats, and of the internal data structures, enabling users to locate any variable or other quantity in which they might be interested. A more detailed summary of these levels can be found in the reference given at the beginning of this section.

6. Summary

The main purpose of this book is to impart a sound knowledge of the use and practice of the FORTRAN programming language. To the extent that any program requires testing and documentation, regardless of the language used, this chapter has set out certain guidelines on these two topics which are generally applicable, but which have been related to FORTRAN wherever possible. References to more detailed studies have been given for those readers who are sufficiently impressed by their importance to be willing to pursue the matter further.

*

This last chapter rounds off the whole book, and with it the topic of programming effectively in a much abused language. It is my sincere hope that it will contribute positively to attempts to improve the general quality of programming in scientific and numerical fields and to ensure that FORTRAN is used well as long as it continues to be used at all.

APPENDIX A: INTRINSIC FUNCTIONS

Intrinsic Function	Definition	Argument Number	Generic Name	Specific Name	Argument Type	Function Type
Type Conversion						
	Conversion to Integer int(*a*) (Note 1)	1	INT	–	Integer	Integer
				INT	Real	Integer
				IFIX	Real	Integer
				IDINT	Double	Integer
				–	Complex	Integer
	Conversion To Real (Note 2)	1	REAL	REAL	Integer	Real
				FLOAT	Integer	Real
				–	Real	Real
				SNGL	Double	Real
				–	Complex	Real
	Conversion to Double (Note 3)	1	DBLE	–	Integer	Double
				–	Real	Double
				–	Double	Double
				–	Complex	Double
	Conversion to Complex (Note 4)	1 or 2	CMPLX	–	Integer	Complex
				–	Real	Complex
				–	Double	Complex
				–	Complex	Complex

	Conversion to Integer (Note 5)	1		ICHAR	Character	Integer
	Conversion to Character (Note 5)	1		CHAR	Integer	Character
Truncation	int(a) (Note 1)	1	AINT	AINT DINT	Real Double	Real Double
Nearest Whole Number	int($a+.5$) if $a \geqslant 0$ int($a-.5$) if $a<0$	1	ANINT	ANINT DNINT	Real Double	Real Double
Nearest Integer	int($a+.5$) if $a \geqslant 0$ int($a-.5$) if $a<0$	1	NINT	NINT IDNINT	Real Double	Integer Integer
Absolute Value	$\lvert a \rvert$ (Note 6) $(ar^2+ai^2)^{1/2}$	1	ABS	IABS ABS DABS CABS	Integer Real Double Complex	Integer Real Double Real
Remaindering	$a_1-\text{int}(a_1/a_2)\ast a_2$ (Note 1)	2	MOD	MOD AMOD DMOD	Integer Real Double	Integer Real Double
Transfer of Sign	$\lvert a_1 \rvert$ if $a_2 \geqslant 0$ $-\lvert a_1 \rvert$ if $a_2 <0$	2	SIGN	ISIGN SIGN DSIGN	Integer Real Double	Integer Real Double
Positive Difference	a_1-a_2 if $a_1>a_2$ 0 if $a_1 \leqslant a_2$	2	DIM	IDIM DIM DDIM	Integer Real Double	Integer Real Double

Double Precision Product					
$a_1 * a_2$	2		DPROD	Real	Double

Choosing Largest Value					
$\max(a_1, a_2, \ldots)$	$\geqslant 2$	MAX	MAX0	Integer	Integer
			AMAX1	Real	Real
			DMAX1	Double	Double
			AMAX0	Integer	Real
			MAX1	Real	Integer

Choosing Smallest Value					
$\min(a_1, a_2, \ldots)$	$\geqslant 2$	MIN	MIN0	Integer	Integer
			AMIN1	Real	Real
			DMIN1	Double	Double
			AMIN0	Integer	Real
			MIN1	Real	Integer

Length					
Length of Character Entity	1		LEN	Character	Integer

Index of a Substring					
Location of Substring a_2 in String a_1 (Note 10)	2		INDEX	Character	Integer

Imaginary Part of Complex Argument					
ai (Note 6)	1		AIMAG	Complex	Real

Conjugate of a						
Complex Argument						
	$(ar, -ai)$	1		CONJG	Complex	Complex
	(Note 6)					

Square Root						
	$(a)^{1/2}$	1	SQRT	SQRT	Real	Real
				DSQRT	Double	Double
				CSQRT	Complex	Complex

Exponential						
	e**a	1	EXP	EXP	Real	Real
				DEXP	Double	Double
				CEXP	Complex	Complex

Natural Logarithm						
	$\log(a)$	1	LOG	ALOG	Real	Real
				DLOG	Double	Double
				CLOG	Complex	Complex

Common Logarithm						
	$\log 10(a)$	1	LOG10	ALOG10	Real	Real
				DLOG10	Double	Double

Sine						
	$\sin(a)$	1	SIN	SIN	Real	Real
				DSIN	Double	Double
				CSIN	Complex	Complex

Cosine						
	$\cos(a)$	1	COS	COS	Real	Real
				DCOS	Double	Double
				CCOS	Complex	Complex

Tangent						
	$\tan(a)$	1	TAN	TAN	Real	Real
				DTAN	Double	Double

Arcsine						
	$\arcsin(a)$	1	ASIN	ASIN	Real	Real
				DASIN	Double	Double

Arccosine

$\arccos(a)$	1	ACOS	ACOS	Real	Real
			DACOS	Double	Double

Arctangent

$\arctan(a)$	1	ATAN	ATAN	Real	Real
			DATAN	Double	Double
$\arctan(a_1/a_2)$	2	ATAN2	ATAN2	Real	Real
			DATAN2	Double	Double

Hyperbolic Sine

$\sinh(a)$	1	SINH	SINH	Real	Real
			DSINH	Double	Double

Hyperbolic Cosine

$\cosh(a)$	1	COSH	COSH	Real	Real
			DCOSH	Double	Double

Hyperbolic Tangent

$\tanh(a)$	1	TANH	TANH	Real	Real
			DTANH	Double	Double

Lexically Greater Than or Equal

$a_1 \geqslant a_2$ (Note 12)	2		LGE	Character	Logical

Lexically Greater Than

$a_1 > a_2$ (Note 12)	2		LGT	Character	Logical

Lexically Less Than or Equal

$a_1 \leqslant a_2$ (Note 12)	2		LLE	Character	Logical

Lexically Less Than

$a_1 < a_2$ (Note 12)	2		LLT	Character	Logical

Notes:

1. For *a* of type iteger, int(*a*) = *a*. For *a* of type real or double precision, there are two cases: if $|a| < 1$ int(*a*) = 0, if $|a| \geq 1$ int(a) is the integer whose magnitude is the largest integer that does not exceed the magnitude of *a* and whose sign is the same as the sign of *a*. For example,

$$\mathrm{int}(-3.7) = -3$$

For *a* of type complex, int(*a*) is the value obtained by applying the above rule to the real part of *a*.

For *a* of type real, IFIX(*a*) is the same as INT(*a*).

2. For *a* of type real, REAL(*a*) is *a*. For *a* of type integer or double precision, REAL(*a*) is as much precision of the significant part of *a* as a real datum can contain. For *a* of type complex, REAL(*a*) is the real part of *a*.

For *a* of type integer, FLOAT(*a*) is the same as REAL(*a*).

3. For *a* of type double precision, DBLE(*a*) is *a*. For *a* of type integer or real, DBLE(*a*) is as much precision of the significant part of *a* as a double precision datum can contain. For *a* of type complex, DBLE(*a*) is as much precision of the significant part of the real part of *a* as a double precision datum can be contain.

4. CMPLX may have one or two arguments. If there is one argument, it may be of type integer, real, double precision, or complex. If there are two arguments, they must both be of the same type and may be of type integer, real, or double precision.

For *a* of type complex, CMPLX(*a*) is *a*. For *a* of type integer, real, or double precision, CMPLX(*a*) is the complex value whose real part is REAL(*a*) and whose imaginary part is zero.

CMPLX(a_1, a_2) is the complex value whose real part is REAL(a_1) and whose imaginary part is REAL(a_2).

5. ICHAR provides a means of converting from a character to an integer, based on the position of the character in the processor collating sequence. The first character in the collating sequence corresponds to position 0 and the last to position $n-1$, where *n* is the number of

characters in the collating sequence.

The value of ICHAR(a) is an integer in the range: $0 \leqslant$ ICHAR(a) $\leqslant$ $n-1$, where a is an argument of type character of length one. The value of a must be a character capable of representation in the processor. The position of that character in the collating sequence is the value of ICHAR.

For any characters c_1 and c_2 capable of reperesentation in the processor, (c_1 .LE. c_2) is true if and only if (ICHAR(c_1) .LE. ICHAR(c_2)) is true, and (c_1 .EQ. c_2) is true if and only if (ICHAR(c_1) .EQ. ICHAR(c_2)) is true.

CHAR(i) returns the character in the ith position of the processor collating sequence. The value is of type character of length one. i must be an integer expression whose value must be in the range $0 \leqslant i \leqslant n-1$.

ICHAR(CHAR(i)) $= i$ for $0 \leqslant i \leqslant n-1$.

CHAR(ICHAR(c)) $= c$ for any character c capable of representation in the processor.

6. A complex value is expressed as an ordered pair of reals, (ar,ai), where ar is the real part and ai is the imaginary part.

7. All angles are expressed in radians.

8. The result of a function of type complex is the principal value.

9. All arguments in an intrinsic function reference must be of the same type.

10. INDEX(a_1,a_2) returns an integer value indicating the starting position within the character string a_1 of a substring identical to string a_2. If a_2 occurs more than once in a_1, the starting position of the first occurence is returned.

If a_2 does not occur in a_1, the value zero is returned. Note that zero is returned in LEN(a_1) $<$ LEN(a_2).

11. The value of the argument of the LEN function need not be defined at the time the function reference is executed.

12. LGE(a_1,a_2) returns the value true if $a_1 = a_2$ or if a_1 follows a_2 in the collating sequence described in American National Standard Code for Information Interchange, ANSI X3.4-1977 (ASCII), and otherwise returns the value false.

LGT(a_1,a_2) returns the value true if a_1 follows a_2 in the collating sequence described in ANSI X3.4-1977 (ASCII), and otherwise returns the value false.

LLE(a_1,a_2) returns the value true if $a_1 = a_2$ or if a_1 preceeds a_2 in the collating sequence described in ANSI X3.4-1977 (ASCII), and otherwise returns the value false.

LLT(a_1,a_2) returns the value true if a_1 precedes a_2 in the collating sequence described in ANSI X3.4-1977 (ASCII), and otherwise returns the value false.

If the operands for LGE, LGT, LLE, and LLT are of unequal length, the shorter operand is considered as if it were extended on the right with blanks to the length of the longer operand.

If either of the character entities being compared contains a character that is not in the ASCII character set, the result is processor-dependent.

Restrictions on Range of Arguments and Results.

Restrictions on the range of arguments and results for intrinsic functions when referenced by their specific names are as follows:

1. Remaindering: The result for MOD, AMOD, and DMOD is undefined when the value of the second argument is zero.

2. Transfer of Sign: If the value of the first argument of ISIGN, SIGN, or DSIGN is zero, the result is zero, which is neither positive or negative (see ANSI, 1978, section 4.1.3).

3. Square Root: The value of the argument of SQRT and DSQRT must be greater than or equal to zero. The result of CSQRT is the principal value with the real part greater than or equal to zero. When the real part of the result is zero, the imaginary part is greater than or equal to zero.

4. Logarithms: The value of the argument of ALOG, DLOG, ALOG10, and DLOG10 must be greater than zero. The value of the argument of CLOG must not be (0.,0.). The range of the imaginary part of the result of CLOG is: $-\pi <$ imaginary part $\leqslant \pi$. The imaginary part of the result is π only when the real part of the argument is less than zero and the imaginary part of the argument is zero.

5. Sine, Cosine, and Tangent: The absolute value of the argument of SIN, DSIN, COS, DCOS, TAN, and DTAN is not restricted to be less than 2π.

6. Arcsine: The absolute value of the argument of ASIN and DASIN must be less than or equal to one. The range of the result is: $-\pi/2 \leqslant$ result $\leqslant \pi/2$.

7. Arccosine: The absolute value of the argument of ACOS and DACOS must be less than or equal to one. The range of the result is: $0 \leqslant$ result $\leqslant \pi$.

8. Arctangent: The range of the result for ATAN and DATAN is: $-\pi/2 \leqslant$ result $\leqslant \pi/2$. If the value of the first argument of ATAN2 or DATAN2 is positive, the result is positive. If the value of the first argument is zero, the result is zero if the second argument is positive and π if the second argument is negative. If the value of the first argument is negative, the result is negative. If the value of the second argument is zero, the absolute value of the result is $\pi/2$. The arguments must not both have the value zero. The range of the result for ATAN2 and DATAN2 is: $-\pi <$ result $\leqslant \pi$.

The above restrictions on arguments and results also apply to the intrinsic functions when referenced by their generic names.

APPENDIX B: FORTRAN STATEMENTS

[ ] indicates optional item

NON-EXECUTABLE STATEMENTS

Program Units

[PROGRAM name]	identifies main program
SUBROUTINE name [(d1,d2....)]	defines name and arguments of subroutine
[type] FUNCTION name ([d1,d2....])	defines type, name and arguments of function
BLOCK DATA [name]	identifies a group of data definitions
ENTRY name [(d1,d2....)]	alternative entry to subroutine or function
function ([d1,d2....]) = exp	statement function — single-line function within a subroutine

Type Declarations

INTEGER a1,a2....	declares type INTEGER
REAL a1,a2....	declares type REAL (floating-point)
LOGICAL a1,a2....	declares type LOGICAL

CHARACTER [*len]a1[*ln1],a2[*ln2]..

declares variables as CHARACTER strings of lengths ln1 etc. with default len (1 if len omitted).

DOUBLE PRECISION a1,a2....

declares type as double-length REAL

COMPLEX a1,a2....

declares complex number of 2 parts

IMPLICIT type (a1,a2....)
      or (a1 − a2)

defines type of variables beginning with letter in range specified

Other Declarations

COMMON [/name/] a1,a2....

names a list of variables or arrays to be shared between program units

DIMENSION a1(i1[,i2..i7]),a2(..)..
    each 'i' is of the form
    [lower bound:] upper bound

defines size and shape of arrays

EQUIVALENCE (a1,a2....)

allows variables to share same location

PARAMETER (name1 = constexp1,name2 = ...)

gives symbolic name to constant expression

EXTERNAL procname1,....

permits external procedure name to be used as an actual argument

INTRINSIC function1,....

permits intrinsic function name to be used as an actual argument

SAVE a1,a2....

allows the named items to retain their values after execution of a RETURN or END statement

    'a's are variable, array or common block names (within / / if common block)

DATA a1,a2.../val1,val2,..../

assigns constant values to named items at compilation time

EXECUTABLE STATEMENTS

variable = expression	arithmetic, logical or character assignment statement; in arithmetic assignment type of expression is converted to type of variable
ASSIGN label TO int	sets statement label to int for use with assigned GO TO
CALL subroutine [(a1,a2....)]	begin execution of named subroutine with actual arguments a1 etc. corresponding to dummy arguments in SUBROUTINE statement
GO TO label	jump to statement label
GO TO (lab1,lab2....) int	jump to lab1 etc. according to value of int
GO TO int [(lab1,lab2....)]	jump to lab1 etc. according to value previously assigned to int in an ASSIGN statement
DO label var = e1,e2[,e3]	loop over following statements until label, var ranges from value of e1 to e2 in steps of e3 (default 1)
IF (logexp) THEN	block IF: following statements obeyed up to ELSE, ELSEIF or ENDIF if logical expression is true
ELSE	following statements obeyed up to ENDIF if logical expression of block IF false
ELSEIF (logexp) THEN	nested block IF: following statements obeyed up to ELSE, ELSEIF or ENDIF if previous block IF logical expression false and current logical expression true
ENDIF	terminates block IF sequence

IF (logexp) statement	logical IF: statement executed if logical expression is true
IF (arithexp) lab1,lab2,lab3	jump to 1st, 2nd or 3rd label if arithmetic expression is <0, $=0$ or >0, respectively
CONTINUE	statement has no effect
PAUSE [num]	causes program to pause until re-started by operator
RETURN [n]	returns control to calling subprogram, optionally n allows return to alternative positions in calling subprogram
END	terminates a program unit
STOP [num]	terminates program, optionally displaying num $(1-5$ digit no. or character string)

Input/Output Statements

READ format label [,I/O list]	read from standard input unit; format label may be replaced by * when format is to be determined by list items (list-directed I/O)
READ (cilist) [I/O list]	general form of read statement; the unit and format specifiers must be present (or *) and in that order; the other items are optional

cilist may contain the items:

    [UNIT =]unit no. (* = standard)
    [FMT =]format lab (* = list-directed)
    REC = record no. (direct access)
    IOSTAT = I/O status (0 = no error,
        + ve = error, − ve = end-of-file)
    ERR = lab (jump to lab if error)
    END = lab (jump to lab if end-of-file)

WRITE (cilist) [I/O list]   general form of write statement
                                             (equivalent to READ)

  cilist same as READ (except END=)

PRINT format label [,I/O list]   write to standard output unit
                                             (equivalent to simple READ)

FORMAT (flist)   controls representation of I/O data
                                             (non-executablc)

  flist is a list of edit descriptors:

    repeatable (may be preceded by a
    constant n for n repetitions)

        Iw   integer value of w posi-
                    tions
        Iw.m   integer value of w posi-
                    tions of which m are
                    always non-blank
        Fw.d   real value of w posi-
                    tions with d decimal
                    places
        Ew.d[Ee]   real value exponent
                    form (e digits in expo-
                    nent)
        Dw.d   double precision value
        Gw.d[Ee]   generalised real value
                    depending on size of
                    value
        Lw   logical value
        A[w]   character value
        nH   string of n characters
                    (Hollerith)

    non-repeatable

        Tc   tabulate to character
                    position c
        TLc   tabulate left by c char-
                    acters
        TRc   tabulate right by c
                    characters
        nX   skip n places to right

/	start new record
:	terminate format scan if no more items in I/O list
kP	scale factor editing
BN or BZ	determine whether blanks interpreted as 0 on input
SP, SS, S	sign printing or suppression

OPEN (olist)

connects a file to user's program and defines its characteristics; the unit no. specification must be present; the others are optional

olist may contain the specifiers:

[UNIT =] unit no.
IOSTAT = I/O status (0 or +ve)
ERR = label (see READ)
FILE = name (or character string)
STATUS = 'OLD' or 'NEW' or 'SCRATCH' or 'UNKNOWN' (default)
ACCESS = 'SEQUENTIAL' (default) or 'DIRECT'
FORM = 'FORMATTED' or 'UNFORMATTED' (default)
RECL = record length (direct access)
BLANK = 'NULL' (default) or 'ZERO' − blanks
   in numeric fields treated as blank or 0

CLOSE (clist)

disconnects a file previously connected by an OPEN statement; the unit no. specifier must be present, the others are optional

clist may contain the specifiers:

[UNIT =]unit no.
IOSTAT = I/O status (see OPEN)
ERR = label
STATUS = 'KEEP' (default) or 'DELETE'

INQUIRE (ilist)

requests information about status or properties a file; enquiry by file or by unit is allowed

ilist may contain the specifiers:

FILE = name
or
[UNIT =] unit no.

and optionally

IOSTAT = I/O status
ERR = label
EXIST = logical variable
OPENED = logical variable
NUMBER = int (set to value of unit no.)
NAMED = logical variable (true if file named)
NAME = character name of file
ACCESS = 'SEQUENTIAL' or 'DIRECT'
SEQUENTIAL = 'YES' or 'NO' or 'UNKNOWN'
DIRECT = 'YES' or 'NO' or 'UNKNOWN'
FORM = 'FORMATTED' or 'UNFORMATTED'
UNFORMATTED = 'YES' or 'NO' or 'UNKNOWN'
RECL = record length (direct access)
NEXTREC = number of next record
BLANK = 'NULL' or 'ZERO'

REWIND (list)   rewinds the file on the given unit

list contains:

[UNIT =]unit no.
and optionally
IOSTAT = I/O status
ERR = label

BACKSPACE (list)   moves file pointer to start of the
                                                 previous record

list is same as for REWIND

ENDFILE (list)   writes an end-of-file mark as next
                                                 record of the file.

list is same as for REWIND

BIBLIOGRAPHY

Aho A.V., Hopcroft J. and Ullman J.D. (1974). "The design and analysis of computer algorithms." Addison-Wesley, Reading, Mass.

ANSI (1978). Programming Language FORTRAN, X3.9-1978, ANSI, New York, (see also p. 217).

Backus J. *et al.* (1957). *In* "Programming Systems and Languages." (S. Rosen, ed.), pp. 29 – 47. McGraw Hill, New York. (1967)

ESA (1982). Software Engineering Handbook, ESA, Darmstadt, W. Germany.

Freeman P. and Wasserman A.I. (1982). "Software Design Techniques." IEEE, New York, N.Y.

Gaggero G. (1983). *In* "Programming for Software Sharing." (D.T. Muxworthy, ed.), pp. 175 – 190. Reidel, Dordrecht, Holland. (1983)

Howden W.E. (1982). "Validation of Scientific Programs." *ACM Computing Surveys* **14**, 2, 193 – 228.

Matthews R. (1984). KAPACK Random Access I/O Using Keywords. CERN Program Library Z303, Geneva, Switzerland.

Metcalf M. (1982). "FORTRAN Optimization." Academic Press, London and New York.

Metcalf M. and Reid J. (1987). "Fortran 8x Explained." Oxford University Press, London and New York.

Myers G. (1979). "The Art of Software Testing." Wiley, New York, N.Y.

Yourdon E. (1980). "Managing the System Life Cycle." Yourdon Inc., New York, N.Y.

SUBJECT INDEX